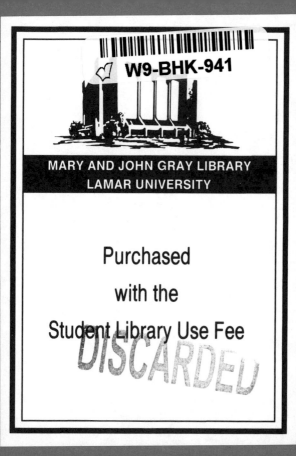

Spelling™

Louisa Moats and Barbara Foorman

Welcome!

Hardcover ISBN 0-590-34489-7
Softcover ISBN 0-590-34465-X

2 3 4 5 6 7 8 9 10   09   03 02 01 00 99 98

Contents

Contents

Contents

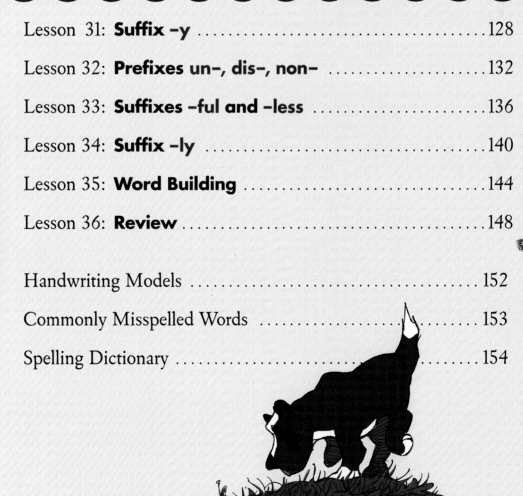

Spelling Strategies
Word Study Path

1. See the word.

START

 See
Look at the letters in the word.

 Say
Say each letter. Then say the word in syllables.

Link
Look for spelling patterns that you know. Group the word with other words like it.

Write
Write the word until you remember how to spell it. Say the letters as you write. Use the word in a sentence.

 Check
Check your spelling word list to see if you spelled the word correctly. Keep your own spelling journal.

4.Write.

Homophones

A See and Say

Spelling Words

tail	steal
tale	steel
pain	higher
pane	hire
waist	groan
waste	grown
wait	shone
weight *LOOKOUT WORD*	shown
peace	toad
piece	towed

Review	Challenge
study	burrow
January	borough
sighed	

My Words

_____

_____

_____

_____

The Spelling Concept

long a	tail	tale
long e	steal	steel
long i	higher	hire
long o	toad	towed

Homophones are words that sound the same but are spelled differently and have different meanings. The vowel sounds in homophones are spelled differently.

B Link Sounds and Letters

Say each spelling word, and listen to the vowel sound. Sort the words according to the long vowel sounds. Underline the letters that spell the long vowel sound. Use a chart like this one.

Buy **pie** by the **piece**.

MEMORY JOGGER

Word Sort

long a	long e	long i	long o

C Write and Check

Which words in the daffynition are homophones? Write them.

_____

_____

DAFFYNITION

What do you call a broken window?

a pane with a pain

Ⓐ Build Vocabulary: **Write the Right Word**

Write the homophones that complete each pair of sentences.

1. A frog's cousin is a _____ .
2. A parked car can be _____ .

3. A storyteller tells a _____ .
4. The dog wags its bushy _____ .

5. Wear a belt around your _____ .
6. Throwing away food is a real _____ .

7. These are the flowers that I have _____ .
8. I let out a sigh and then a _____ .

9. The pie was fresh, and I cut a _____ .
10. What I like is quiet and _____ .

Spell Chat

Challenge a classmate to think of two other **homophone** pairs with long vowel sounds, such as *tow* and *toe*.

Ⓑ Word Study: **Letter Patterns**

Read each phrase. Change the underlined letter or letters in each word to create a spelling word that rhymes and makes sense in the phrase. Write the spelling word.

11. climb <u>s</u>igher
12. a heavy <u>fr</u>eight
13. sparkled and <u>l</u>one
14. a long, boring <u>g</u>ait
15. presented or <u>b</u>lown

16. a taxi for <u>t</u>ire
17. window <u>cr</u>ane
18. a real <u>squ</u>eal
19. a metal called <u>kn</u>eel
20. an ache or <u>br</u>ain

Ⓒ Write

Write two sentences. In each sentence use a pair of homophones.

_____

_____

_____

Be a Spelling Sleuth
Look for book titles at home, in the library, and in bookstores that contain a homophone with a long vowel sound, such as *eight* and *peace*. Keep a list.

Spelling Words

tail	steal
tale	steel
pain	higher
pane	hire
waist	groan
waste	grown
wait	shone
weight (LOOKOUT WORD)	shown
peace	toad
piece	towed

Review	Challenge
study	burrow
January	borough
sighed	

My Words

_____

_____

_____

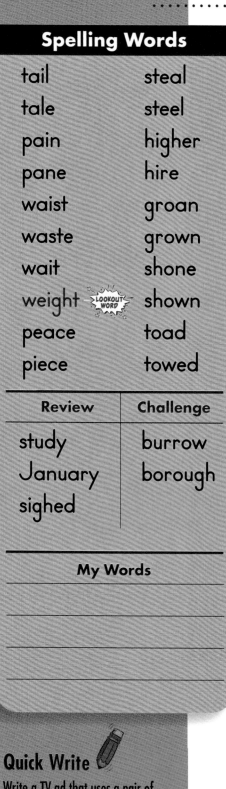

Spelling Words

tail	steal
tale	steel
pain	higher
pane	hire
waist	groan
waste	grown
wait	shone
weight *LOOKOUT WORD*	shown
peace	toad
piece	towed

Review	Challenge
study	burrow
January	borough
sighed	

My Words

Quick Write

Write a TV ad that uses a pair of homophones to sell a product or service. Use two spelling words.

A Write a Dialogue

You may wish to do this activity on a computer.

Write a conversation between two characters in which they talk about something that happened. Use at least three spelling words. Remember to use quotation marks around the words the characters say.

B Proofread

Pia wrote a dialogue that didn't make sense because she used three homophones incorrectly. She also misspelled one word and made one punctuation mistake. Find and correct her mistakes.

Tip
An apostrophe takes the place of letters left out in contractions.

"What really happened on January 3?" asked Dina.

"Its quite a tail," replied Shaquille. "My family went to a football game. Unfortunately, our car was toad. You should have heard us groan! Fortunately, the sun shone all afternoon, because we had to weight for four hours to get the car back!"

Dina laughed.

"Next time you'll walk!"

PROOFREADING MARKS
∧ Add
⊙ Add a period
ℓ Take out
↻ Move
≡ Capital letter
/ Small letter
¶ Indent paragraph

Now proofread your conversation. Check for spelling, punctuation, and the correct use of apostrophes in contractions.

Ⓐ Use the Dictionary: Alphabetical Order

All dictionary entries are in alphabetical order. When two words begin with the same letter, the second letter is used to put the words in alphabetical order.

Write each group of words in alphabetical order.
Use the Spelling Dictionary to check your list.

tale	groan	piece		peace	toad	weight
wait	apple	find		tail	pane	waste

_____   _____

_____   _____

_____   _____

_____   _____

_____   _____

_____   _____

Ⓑ Test Yourself

The vowels in each of your spelling words are written in code. Use the decoder to figure out each word. Write the spelling word.

a = %   e = *   i = ^   o = #

1. t%^l   6. p%n*   11. p%^n   16. h^gh*r
2. sh#n*   7. w%^st   12. h^r*   17. t#w*d
3. gr#wn   8. st**l   13. w%st*   18. gr#%n
4. t%l*   9. w*^ght   14. p^*c*   19. p*%c*
5. t#%d   10. st*%l   15. w%^t   20. sh#wn

For Tomorrow...

Get ready to share the **homophones** that you discovered, and remember to study for your test!

Get Word Wise

The word *weight* comes from an Old English word that means "to carry." Of course, anything that you carry— from a piece of paper to a pack full of school books— has weight.

Word Study Strategy

See the word

START

Say it slowly

Link sounds and letters

Write

Check

END

Spelling Words

pause
paws
allowed
aloud
chews
choose
root
route *LOOKOUT WORD*
bear
bare

hair
hare
bored
board
coarse
course
hoarse
horse
fur
fir

Review	Challenge
weight	foreword
barefoot	forward
pair	

My Words

More Homophones

A See and Say

The Spelling Concept

allowed	hair	fur
aloud	hare	fir

Homophones are words that sound the same but are spelled differently and have different meanings. The difference between the words in many homophone pairs is in the way the vowel sound is spelled.

Look, two o's in choose!

MEMORY JOGGER

B Link Sounds and Letters

Say each spelling word. Listen carefully to the vowel sound. Sort the homophones on a chart like this one.

Word Sort

/ô/ as in jaw	/ou/ as in shout	/ōō/ as in boot	/âr/ as in care	/ôr/ as in wore	/ûr/ as in blur

C Write and Check

Which words in the riddle are homophones? Write the words from your spelling list.

_____

_____

_____

_____

RIDDLE
What do you call a rabbit's fur?

hare hair, of course

Vocabulary Practice

Ⓐ Build Vocabulary: Word Meaning

Write the correct homophone for each underlined definition.

fir	root	aloud	hare	chews
route	allowed	hair	choose	fur

Shh! Talking **(1. out loud)** is not **(2. permitted)**.

I like to **(3. select)** the treats my new puppy **(4. grinds between his teeth)**.

Does a **(5. animal like a large rabbit)** have **(6. strands that grow on your head)**? No, it has fur.

The rabbit's white **(7. soft, thick, coat)** stood out against the tall **(8. tree)**.

A giant tree **(9. part of a plant or tree)** blocked the jogger's **(10. road or path)**.

> **Spell Chat**
> Name a **homophone** pair. Ask a friend to make up a sentence that uses the two **homophones**.

Ⓑ Word Study: Context Clues

Answer each question with a homophone phrase. Use the spelling words below.

board	paws	bored	bare	horse
coarse	course	bear	hoarse	pause

What do you call a pony with a sore throat? a ___11___ ___12___

What is a rough road? a ___13___ ___14___

What can you call a surfboard that hasn't been used for a long time? a ___15___ ___16___

What do you call "rest for an active puppy"? a ___17___ ___18___

What is a grizzly without any fur? a ___19___ ___20___

Spelling Words

pause	hair
paws	hare
allowed	bored
aloud	board
chews	coarse
choose	course
root	hoarse
route	horse
bear	fur
bare	fir

Review	Challenge
weight	foreword
barefoot	forward
pair	

My Words

_____

_____

_____

_____

_____

Spelling Words

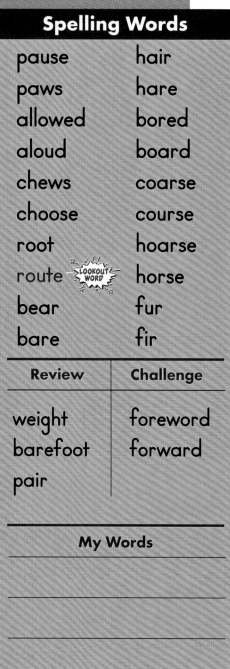

pause	hair
paws	hare
allowed	bored
aloud	board
chews	coarse
choose	course
root	hoarse
route *LOOKOUT WORD*	horse
bear	fur
bare	fir

Review	Challenge
weight	foreword
barefoot	forward
pair	

My Words

Quick Write

Write a sentence, using as many homophone spelling words as you can.

You may wish to write your letter on a computer.

Ⓐ Write a Letter

What would you think if you received a letter from a friend that began, "Yesterday in the forest I saw a pair of huge paws resting on a log." You'd want to read more, wouldn't you? Begin a letter with those words, and finish it in an amazing way.

Ⓑ Proofread

Leo wrote a letter to his friend. He used four homophones incorrectly. He also made one punctuation and two capitalization errors. Correct the errors.

Tip
Capitalize the pronoun *I* whenever you use it in place of your name.

July 10, 1998

Dear Benji,

Yesterday in the forest, I saw a pare of huge paws resting on a log. my hare stood on end. The pause looked like large pillows covered with fir. Then I looked up. There was the biggest bear I had ever seen. I guess it was as surprised as i was, because it took off Lucky me!

Leo

PROOFREADING MARKS

∧ Add
⊙ Add a period
ℓ Take out
↻ Move
≡ Capital letter
╱ Small letter
¶ Indent paragraph

Now proofread your letter. Check for spelling, punctuation, capitalization, and the correct use of homophones.

Get Word Wise

Horses are known for running swiftly and gracefully. It makes sense that the word *horse* comes from the Latin word *cursus*, which means "running." The word *horse* does not look much like the word *cursus*. However, the word *courser*, another name for a spirited horse, does.

Ⓐ Use the Dictionary: Alphabetical Order

Words in a dictionary are arranged in alphabetical order. When two words begin with the same letter, the second letter is used to put the words in alphabetical order. If the words also have the same second letter, the third letter is used. Write these words in alphabetical order. Use the Spelling Dictionary to check your list.

fir	choose	board	course	hair	bare
bored	fur	chews	horse	bear	coarse

_____

_____

_____

_____

_____

_____

_____

_____

_____

_____

_____

_____

Word Study Strategy

See the word

START

Say it slowly

Link sounds and letters

Write

Check

END

Ⓑ Test Yourself

Write the word for each clue. Then write its homophone.

1-2. a short rest

3-4. a rabbit

5-6. without covering

7-8. an underground plant part

9-10. a cut piece of wood

11-12. a kind of tree

13-14. rough

15-16. able to be heard

17-18. to select

19-20. a large animal

For Tomorrow...
Get ready to share the **homophones** you found, and remember to study for your test!

Spelling Words

eager
repeat
meal
feast
least
measles
please
pleasant
lead *LOOKOUT WORD*
ahead

bread
instead
spread
steady
ready
already
feather
weather
breakfast
health

Review	Challenge
route	eavesdrop
what's	wealthy
clear	

My Words

Long e or Short e? Words With ea

A See and Say

The Spelling Concept

long e	feast	lead
short e	bread	lead

The letters *ea* can be used to spell /ē/ or /e/. In some words, the letters can be used to spell both sounds.

B Link Sounds and Letters

Say each spelling word. Listen to the vowel sound spelled *ea*. Then fill in the diagram to sort the spelling words. Which word belongs in the middle?

Look out for **ea**: a l**ea**d pencil, l**ea**d a band.

MEMORY JOGGER

Word Sort

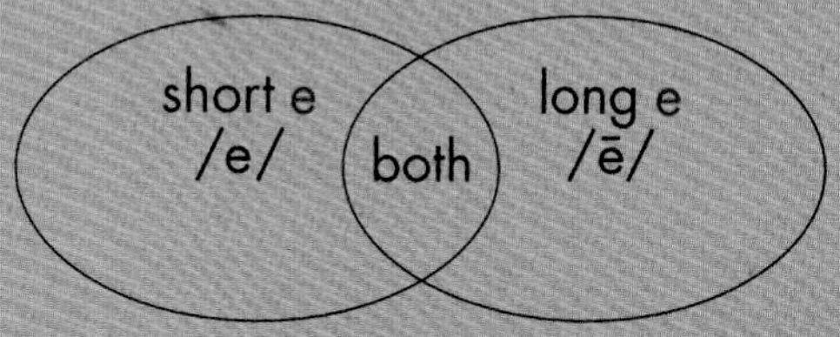

short e
/e/

both

long e
/ē/

C Write and Check

Write the spelling words in the poem.

_____

_____

_____

_____

JAN'S FAVORITE FOODS

For breakfast, it's bread with a honey spread.
A feast is a lunch of berries to munch.
Dinner is a treat of peas and meat.

A Build Vocabulary: **Antonyms**

Antonyms are words that have opposite meanings, such as *asleep* and *awake*. Write a spelling word that is the opposite of each phrase.

1. not behind, but _____
2. not shaky, but _____
3. not most, but _____
4. not sickness, but _____
5. not follow, but _____
6. not unpleasant, but _____

Spell Chat

Say a sentence that is the opposite of what you really mean. For example, "I like to be last in line for lunch." Have a friend suggest what you really mean.

B Word Study: **Word Clues**

Use the clues to write spelling words. Circle the letters *ea* when they spell long *e*. Underline the letters *ea* when they spell short *e*.

7. breakfast, lunch, or dinner
8. part of a sandwich
9. all set to go
10. a huge fancy dinner
11. very willing
12. to make happy
13. put on butter or jelly
14. say again
15. found on a bird

16. before now
17. something cloudy or fair
18. in place of
19. a spotty disease
20. first meal of the day
21. a gray metal

C Write

Write a short weather report. Use these words.

weather   pleasant   clear   ready

_____

_____

Spelling Words

eager	bread
repeat	instead
meal	spread
feast	steady
least	ready
measles	already
please	feather
pleasant	weather
lead	breakfast
ahead	health

Review	Challenge
route	eavesdrop
what's	wealthy
clear	

LOOKOUT WORD

My Words

_____

_____

_____

_____

Spelling Words

eager	bread
repeat	instead
meal	spread
feast	steady
least	ready
measles	already
please	feather
pleasant	weather
lead *LOOKOUT WORD*	breakfast
ahead	health

Review	Challenge
route	eavesdrop
what's	wealthy
clear	

My Words

Quick Write

Use two spelling words and other words with *ea* to write a description of something delicious you would like to spread on your breakfast bread one morning.

A Write a Conversation

 You may wish to do this activity on a computer.

Imagine you are a waiter or waitress in a restaurant. Write the beginning of a conversation between you and a customer. Use at least four spelling words.

B Proofread

Tony wrote this conversation. He made two spelling errors and one error in subject-verb agreement. He also made two errors in punctuation. Correct the errors.

Tip
Check your sentences to make sure that all your subjects and verbs agree.

Waiter: Good morning! Are you redy to order?

Customer: Whats good?

Waiter: The breakfast special is good.

Customer: I'm not sure if I want such a big meal

Waiter: The breakfast special is already ready.

Customer: Maybe I'll have pancakes.

Waiter: Sir, the breakfast special are the only meal we have!

Customer: One breakfast special, pleese!

PROOFREADING MARKS

∧ Add
⊙ Add a period
ℓ Take out
◡∧ Move
≡ Capital letter
／ Small letter
¶ Indent paragraph

Now proofread your conversation. Check for spelling and punctuation errors, and subject-verb agreement.

Ⓐ Use the Dictionary: Guide Words

Guide words are found at the top of each dictionary page. The first guide word is the first word on the page. The second guide word is the last word on the page. The other words on the page are listed in alphabetical order between the guide words.

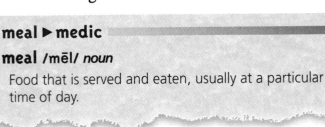

meal ▶ medic

meal /mēl/ *noun*
Food that is served and eaten, usually at a particular time of day.

medic /med ik/ *noun*
Someone trained to give medical help in an emergency.

Look up the spelling words in your Spelling Dictionary. Write the guide words for each.

health _____

feast _____

please _____

spread _____

Ⓑ Test Yourself

The letters *ea* are missing from each spelling word. Write the words correctly, adding *ea* to each one.

1. ml	**6.** ger	**11.** fther	**16.** fst
2. instd	**7.** wther	**12.** ahd	**17.** sprd
3. ld	**8.** hlth	**13.** brd	**18.** plse
4. plsant	**9.** stdy	**14.** rept	**19.** rdy
5. alrdy	**10.** msles	**15.** brkfast	**20.** lst

For Tomorrow...
Get ready to share your **ea** words related to cooking, and remember to study for your test!

Get Word Wise

When you hear the word *weather*, do you think of sunny days or storms? In ancient times, people must have been more interested in wind. How do we know this? Our modern word *weather* came from the Anglo-Saxon word *weder*, which meant "to blow."

Word Study Strategy

See the word

Say it slowly

Link sounds and letters

Write

Check

Spelling Words

found
sound
round
pound
count
amount
account *LOOKOUT WORD*
bounce
pounce
owl

howl
frown
downtown
crowd
drowsy
towel
tower
shower
power
powder

Review	Challenge
lead	astounding
beginning	announce
couch	

My Words

Words With ou or ow

A See and Say

The Spelling Concept

found   frown

count   crowd

The letters ow and ou usually stand for /ou/.

B Link Sounds and Letters

Say each spelling word. Listen for /ou/, and look at the letters that spell that sound. Then sort the spelling words on a chart like this.

One sound, two spellings: Owls howl loud sounds.

MEMORY JOGGER

Word Sort

___ou___	ow___	___ow___	___ow___ow___

C Write and Check

In which words in the rhyming riddle do you hear /ou/? Write the spelling words.

RHYME TIME
What does a wise bird use after taking a shower?

an owl towel

Vocabulary Practice

Ⓐ Build Vocabulary: Action Verbs

The action words are missing from the rhymes. Write a spelling word to complete each sentence.

1. Balls ____.
2. Cats ____.
3. Carpenters ____.
4. Lost things are ____.
5. Sad people ____.
6. Astronauts ____ down.
7. Skyscrapers ____.
8. Raindrops ____.

Ⓑ Word Study: Analogies

The second pair of words in each sentence go together in the same way as the first pair. Write the spelling word that completes each analogy.

9. *Cow* is to *herd*, as *person* is to ____.
10. *Pound* is to *hammer*, as *dry* is to ____.
11. *Near* is to *far*, as *uptown* is to ____.
12. *Wide-awake* is to *alert*, as *sleepy* is to ____.
13. *Dog* is to *poodle*, as *bird* is to ____.
14. *Block* is to *square*, as *ball* is to ____.
15. *See* is to *light*, as *hear* is to ____.
16. *Fast* is to *quick*, as *total* is to ____.
17. *Cat* is to *meow*, as *wolf* is to ____.

Ⓒ Write

Write a sentence, using the spelling words *account*, *powder*, and *power*.

_____

_____

> **Spell Chat**
> Challenge the person next to you to use as many spelling words as possible in the same sentence.

Be a Spelling Sleuth

Be on the lookout for names of streets that have *ou* or *ow* in them, such as South Street or Crown Lane. Keep a list.

Spelling Words

found	howl
sound	frown
round	downtown
pound	crowd
count	drowsy
amount	towel
account *LOOKOUT WORD*	tower
bounce	shower
pounce	power
owl	powder

Review	Challenge
lead	astounding
beginning	announce
couch	

My Words

_____

_____

_____

_____

You may wish to do this activity on a computer.

Spelling Words

found	howl
sound	frown
round	downtown
pound	crowd
count	drowsy
amount	towel
account	tower
bounce	shower
pounce	power
owl	powder

account — LOOKOUT WORD

Review	Challenge
lead	astounding
beginning	announce
couch	

My Words

Quick Write

Describe a funny problem and a solution.

Ⓐ Write an Advice Column

Imagine that you write an advice column for a newspaper. A reader asks you for tips on how to best do homework. Write some advice. Use at least three spelling words.

Ⓑ Proofread

Beth wrote this advice for her column. She made one punctuation error, one capitalization error, and three spelling errors. Correct them.

Tip

Remember to use a period at the end of each declarative sentence.

Dear Angela,

    Do your homework in a quiet place It's hard to think when there's a crowd arownd you. sit up straight at your desk, so that you don't become drousy. When you're first begining, go over the amount of work you have, and plan your time well. I hope these tips are helpful.

                    Good luck,
                    Beth

PROOFREADING MARKS

∧ Add
⊙ Add a period
ℓ Take out
⌒∧ Move
≡ Capital letter
/ Small letter
¢ Indent paragraph

Now proofread your letter for spelling, punctuation, and capitalization.

A Use the Dictionary: Guide Words

At the top of each dictionary page, you'll find guide words. They tell the first and last words on that page.

> **crop ▶ crown**
>
> **crop** /krop/ *noun* A plant grown in large amounts, usually for food.

Write the spelling word that goes on the page with the guide words above. _____

Write the spelling words that go on the same page as these guide words. Look in the Spelling Dictionary to check your work.

harmful • hungry _____

physical • powder _____

B Test Yourself

Complete each phrase or sentence with a spelling word. The first letter is a clue.

1. a coyote's h___
2. to b___ a ball
3. use baby p___
4. an angry f___
5. an April s___
6. people in a c___
7. a charge a___
8. a beach t___
9. a d___ street
10. c___ your money

11. lost and f___
12. Sh! Don't make a s___.
13. an a___ of money
14. tired and d___
15. p___ a nail
16. a castle t___
17. a wise old o___
18. A circle is r___.
19. electric p___
20. cats p___

For Tomorrow...
*Get ready to share the words with **ou** or **ow** that you discovered, and remember to study for your test!*

Get Word Wise

Everyone thinks that an owl says, "Who-o-o, who-o-o." However, have you ever heard the sound an owl really makes at night? If so, you know that owls howl. That's why the name of this wise-looking bird comes from the Latin verb *ululare*, which means "to howl."

Word Study Strategy

See the word

START

Say it slowly

Link sounds and letters

Write

Check

END

Words With ou and ough

Ⓐ See and Say

Spelling Words

county	enough
country	double
bought	trouble
brought	dough
fought	though
thought	thorough
ought	through
cough	doubt **LOOKOUT WORD**
rough	drought
tough	throughout

Review	Challenge
account	thoroughfare
used	bough
cloud	

My Words

The Spelling Concept

double
county

ought
though
through
drought

The letters *ou* and *ough* are used to spell many different sounds.

Don't dou**b**t me! Add a **b**!

MEMORY JOGGER

Ⓑ Link Sounds and Letters

Say each spelling word. Listen for the vowel sounds that are spelled by *ou* and *ough*. Sort the spelling words on a chart like this one. (You will write one word twice.)

Word Sort

vowel sound in paw	vowel sound in stuff	vowel sound in toe	vowel sound in do	vowel sound in shout

Ⓒ Write and Check

Read the joke. Write the spelling words that are in it.

_____

_____

JOKE
Why did the baker stop making bread?
She wasn't making enough dough.

Vocabulary Practice

Ⓐ Build Vocabulary: **Synonyms**

A synonym is a word or phrase that has the same or nearly the same meaning as another word. Write a spelling word that is a synonym for each word or phrase.

1. a nation
2. strong
3. twice as much
4. careful
5. should
6. a flour paste
7. even if
8. done
9. right amount
10. lack of rain
11. a sound to clear the throat
12. to not be sure
13. difficulty

Ⓑ Word Study: **Irregular Verbs**

Some past-tense verbs are irregular. They do not end in *ed*. Complete each sentence by writing the past tense of the verb in ( ).

14. We (bring) home three small kittens.
15. The kittens played and (fight) with each other.
16. We (buy) them special kitten food.
17. We all (think) the kittens were so cute!

Ⓒ Write

Write two sentences about taking a trip. Use these spelling words.

throughout   rough   cloud   county

_____

_____

_____

Be a Spelling Sleuth

Look on labels of items you see in supermarkets for *ou* and *ough* words such as *dough, thoroughly,* and *cough syrup.* Keep a list.

Spell Chat

Challenge a classmate to think of four more words with *ou* as in *county,* and use them in a sentence.

Spelling Words

county	enough
country	double
bought	trouble
brought	dough
fought	though
thought	thorough
ought	through
cough	doubt
rough	drought
tough	throughout

Review	Challenge
account	thoroughfare
used	bough
cloud	

My Words

_____

_____

_____

_____

Words With *ou* and *ough* **25**

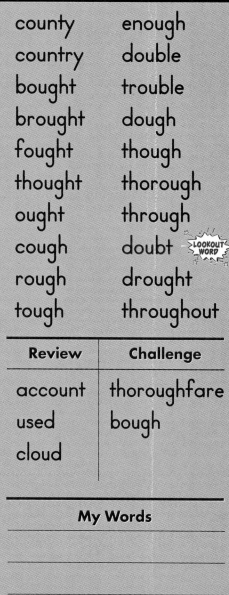

Spelling Words

county	enough
country	double
bought	trouble
brought	dough
fought	though
thought	thorough
ought	through
cough	doubt
rough	drought
tough	throughout

Review	Challenge
account	thoroughfare
used	bough
cloud	

My Words

Quick Write

Use three words with *ou* and *ough* in a short description of someplace you have visited.

 You may wish to do this activity on a computer.

Ⓐ Write a Journal Entry

You can write about events in your life in a journal. Think about something important that has happened to you in the last year. Maybe you moved. Maybe you decided to try something new. In a journal entry, tell about this event. Use three or more spelling words.

Ⓑ Proofread

Here is Jim's journal. It has four spelling errors and one punctuation error. Jim also forgot to indent a paragraph. Help him correct his errors.

Tip
Remember to indent the first word of each paragraph.

> Last summer was a tuff time for me. My family moved from the city to the contry. I felt sad. I was ust to spending time with my pals.
> When school started, though, my ideas changed. I made a lot of new friends. I still miss the city, but there's no dout I will like living here, too

PROOFREADING MARKS

∧ Add
⊙ Add a period
ℓ Take out
⌒ Move
≡ Capital letter
/ Small letter
¶ Indent paragraph

Now proofread your journal entry for spelling and punctuation. Be sure you indented each paragraph.

Ⓐ Use the Dictionary: Dictionary Entry

A dictionary entry tells you how many syllables a word has and how it is pronounced. An entry also gives parts of speech, definitions, and example sentences. Read the following dictionary entry.

> **coun•try** /kun trē/ *noun*
> 1. A part of the world with its own borders and government.
> 2. Undeveloped land away from towns or cities.
> 3. The people of a nation. *The president asked for the country's help.* ▸ *noun,* **plural countries**

How many syllables are in the word *country*? _____

What part of speech is *country*? _____

Read the sample sentence. Now write a sentence for another meaning of the word.

_____

Ⓑ Test Yourself

Write the spelling word hidden in each group of letters.

1. xrbroughtsu
2. mdthoroughya
3. avdoubletom
4. oughtjron
5. kcountrylus
6. throughoutzslm
7. yroughmel
8. throughmly
9. rokcountyp
10. zydoughful
11. troublebis
12. sfoughtwns
13. orstenough
14. lyboughtir
15. thoughnlys
16. respdoubt
17. bmtoughd
18. chlcoughr
19. thoughtwhm
20. droughtlebx

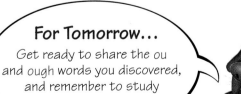

For Tomorrow...
Get ready to share the ou and ough words you discovered, and remember to study for your test.

Get Word Wise

The word *double* comes from two old words that meant *two* and *fold*. Together they make the word *twofold*, the meaning of *double*. Today we use the word *double* in many different ways. Have you ever jumped *double-Dutch* or *double-checked* your work? Think of some other *double* expressions.

Word Study Strategy

See the word

START

Say it slowly

Link sounds and letters

Write

Check

END

The Wolf and the Drought

Complete each sentence with a spelling word.

meal   drought   repeat   weather   howl

One night during dinner Juan heard the (1) of a wolf. "Why do wolves do that?" he asked his grandfather. Grandfather finished eating his (2) and said, "I'll tell you a story my grandfather told to me." Then he began to (3) the tale he had heard many years before.

"Long ago the (4) was endlessly hot. The people hadn't seen rain for nearly a year. A terrible (5) scorched the land.

powder   doubt   instead   country   shower

"**T**he soil was as dry as (6) . The wild animals throughout the (7) were searching for water. There was no (8) that rain was needed soon. One day a young wolf started howling (9) of barking. Then suddenly there was a heavy rain (10) .

spread   already   though   thought   brought

"**B**y evening, the rivers and lakes were (11) filled with water. Some people (12) that the young wolf's howling had (13) the rain. The story of the young wolf (14) far and wide. Even (15) some did not believe the story, they were happy that it was raining. To this day, many people look up at the sky expecting rain whenever they hear a howling wolf."

Pyramid Puzzles

Each word in the pyramid has one more letter than the word above it. Add a letter to the second word to make the third word. The letter may be added at the beginning or in the middle of the word.

1.

eat
east

_ _ _ _ _

2.

count
county

_ _ _ _ _ _

3.

fun
fund

_ _ _ _ _

4.

once
ounce

_ _ _ _ _ _

5.

ad
tad

_ _ _ _ _

(pyramid answers shown: toad, country, found, least, pounce)

Related Words

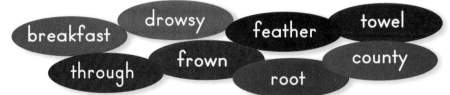

breakfast · drowsy · feather · towel · frown · county · through · root

Read each group of words, and think about how the words are alike. Then write a spelling word that belongs to the group.

6. flower, leaf, _____

7. lunch, dinner, _____

8. smile, scowl, _____

9. sponge, mop, _____

10. tired, sleepy, _____

11. finished, completed, _____

12. town, state, _____

13. beak, wing, _____

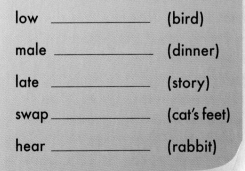

Anagrams

Anagrams are words that have the same letters but not in the same order. *Horse* is an anagram for *shore*.

Write the spelling word that is an anagram for each word below. There is a clue in ( ).

low _____ (bird)

male _____ (dinner)

late _____ (story)

swap _____ (cat's feet)

hear _____ (rabbit)

Advertise It

Ads encourage you to buy and try new things. Here's an ad for a new cereal. *Choose Wheat Crunchies for breakfast. You can't start the day a better way.* Write an ad for these products. Use two or more spelling words in each.

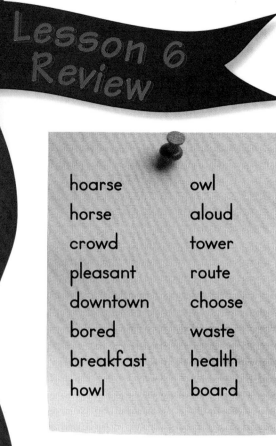

hoarse	owl
horse	aloud
crowd	tower
pleasant	route
downtown	choose
bored	waste
breakfast	health
howl	board

1. a funny movie about a clever animal

_____

_____

2. a new adventure book that takes place in a city

_____

_____

3. a book of new elephant jokes

_____

_____

4. a TV show about eating good food

_____

_____

5. a computer game about an astronaut

_____

_____

Tip
Remember to end each sentence with the correct punctuation.

Look back at My Words and the words you misspelled in your Unit 1 Posttests. Use them to write another ad.

6. a catchy new song

_____

_____

PROOFREADING MARKS
∧ Add
⊙ Add a period
ℓ Take out
↶↷ Move
≡ Capital letter
/ Small letter
¶ Indent paragraph

Review It

Choose a product from above and write a short review of it for a consumer magazine. Tell why you do or don't like it. Proofread for spelling, capitalization, and punctuation.

Write It Right!

Write the homophone that completes each sentence.

toad   towed

1. Our truck was _____ to the garage.

2. The garage sign had a picture of a large, brown _____ on it.

allowed   aloud

3. I called Eric's name _____ .

4. Someone said, "Quiet please! Talking is not _____ ."

wait   weight

5. What's the _____ of this pumpkin?

6. I can't _____ to see if it wins a prize.

peace   piece

7. After dinner, I will eat a _____ of fruit.

8. At nighttime, we have _____ and quiet.

groan   grown

9. Dad said, "Ms. Jones is knitting three socks for Jay because he's _____ another foot."

10. I always _____ when Dad makes a bad joke.

chews   choose

11. My puppy always _____ on my sneaker.

12. I wish she would _____ a bone instead.

Spelling Matters!

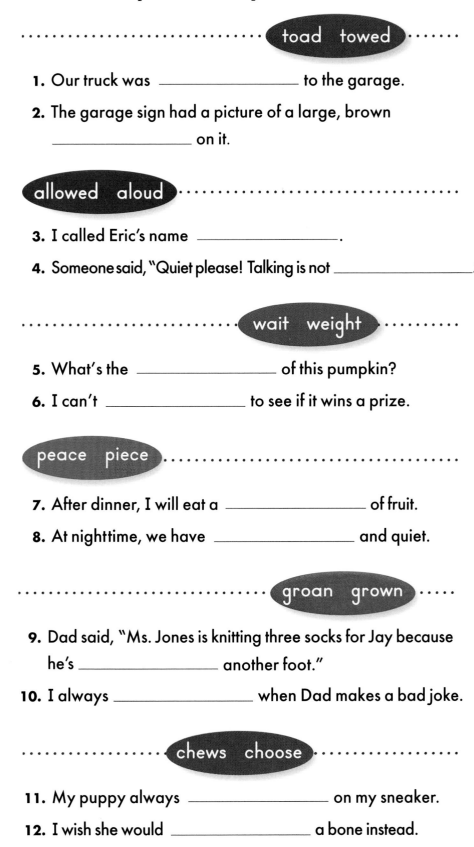

Unusual Letter Pairs: kn and qu

LESSON 7

Spelling Words

knee	quilt
knot	quite
knock	quiet
know	queen
knife	quarter
knight	question
knuckles	square
quack	squeeze
quick	squeak
quit	squirrel

LOOKOUT WORD

Review	Challenge
doubt	knowledge
worried	equality
guess	

My Words

Ⓐ See and Say

The Spelling Concept

kn	know	knife
qu	quack	squirrel

The letters *kn* stand for /n/ as in *knight*. The *k* is silent.
The letters *qu* stand for /kw/ as in *quit*. The letter *q* is always followed by *u*.

U and I eat when it's quiet.

MEMORY JOGGER

Ⓑ Link Sounds and Letters

Say each spelling word. Listen for /n/ or /kw/ at the beginning of each word. Then sort the words on webs like these.

Word Sort

/n/

/kw/

Ⓒ Write and Check

Write the spelling words that are in the joke.

_____

_____

_____

JOKE

What do you get when you cross a quick squirrel and a quiet kangaroo?

an animal that carries nuts in its pocket.

Vocabulary Practice

Ⓐ Build Vocabulary: **Classifying**

Think about how each set of words goes together.
Then write a spelling word that belongs to each group.

1. chipmunk, rabbit, ___
2. foot, ankle, ___
3. tap, bang, ___
4. spoon, fork, ___
5. hands, fingers, ___
6. fast, rapid, ___
7. castle, horse, ___
8. really, very, ___
9. silent, noiseless, ___
10. nickel, dime, ___
11. statement, exclamation, ___

12. triangle, circle, ___
13. king, princess, ___
14. blanket, sheet, ___
15. tie, tangle, ___
16. pinch, press, ___

> **Spell Chat**
> Challenge your neighbor to think of four words with **qu**, and to use each word in a sentence.

Ⓑ Word Study: **Irregular Verbs**

Most past-tense verbs end in *ed*.
Verbs that don't follow this pattern are irregular. Write the present tense of each past-tense verb that is underlined. Circle the verbs that are irregular.

17. The barn doors <u>squeaked</u> when I opened them.

18. I <u>knew</u> someone or something was inside.

19. Then two large ducks <u>quacked</u> loudly from the hay loft.

20. I <u>quit</u> being afraid and began to laugh.

Ⓒ Write

Use these words to write a tongue twister.

queen   quick   quiet

___

Be a Spelling Sleuth

Look at product labels in supermarkets and dime stores for words with kn and qu. Make a list of the words you find, such as *quarter, knitting yarn,* and *squid.*

Spelling Words	
knee	quilt
knot	quite
knock	quiet
know	queen
knife	quarter
knight	question
knuckles	square
quack	squeeze
quick	squeak
quit	squirrel

Review	Challenge
doubt	knowledge
worried	equality
guess	

My Words

___

___

___

___

Spelling Words

knee	quilt
knot	quite
knock	quiet 
know	queen
knife	quarter
knight	question
knuckles	square
quack	squeeze
quick	squeak
quit	squirrel

Review	Challenge
doubt	knowledge
worried	equality
guess	

My Words

_____

_____

_____

Quick Write

Write a funny sentence with at least four spelling words.

You may wish to do this activity on a computer.

A Write a Paragraph

Write a paragraph about an idea you have for a new gadget or machine. Tell what your invention will do and how it works. Use at least three spelling words.

B Proofread

Aaron wrote a paragraph about his idea for an invention. He made four spelling errors and left out an exclamation mark.

Tip

Use exclamation marks only to show strong feelings.

> Did you ever try to tie a not at the end of a balloon? If you have, then you know this can be qite hard to do. My brilliant idea is to invent a machine that ties the knot for you. It would be quick and easy to use. You just sqeeze the end of the balloon, place it in the machine, and your balloon is tied.
> Oops, I gues you still have to remember not to let go

PROOFREADING MARKS

∧ Add
⊙ Add a period
ℓ Take out
⟳ Move
≡ Capital letter
／ Small letter
¢ Indent paragraph

Now proofread your paragraph. Check your spelling, capitalization, and punctuation.

Ⓐ Use the Dictionary: **Example Sentence**

A dictionary entry may give an example sentence to help you understand the meaning of a word. Read the dictionary entry for *quiet*.

> **qui·et** /kwī it/
> 1. *adjective* Not loud. *I spoke in a quiet voice.*
> 2. *adjective* Peaceful and calm. *We spent a quiet afternoon by the river.*
> 3. *noun* The state of being quiet. *The teacher asked for quiet.*

Write another example sentence for each meaning.

_____

_____

_____

Ⓑ Test Yourself

Write the spelling word that rhymes with each word. Make sure the spelling word ends with the underlined letters.

1. ri<u>ght</u>
2. thr<u>ee</u>
3. <u>ch</u>uckles
4. st<u>ilt</u>
5. sp<u>ot</u>
6. w<u>eak</u>
7. r<u>ock</u>
8. s<u>een</u>
9. <u>tr</u>ack
10. l<u>ife</u>
11. sl<u>ow</u>
12. st<u>ick</u>
13. d<u>iet</u>
14. po<u>rter</u>
15. sh<u>are</u>
16. gr<u>it</u>
17. qua<u>rrel</u>
18. br<u>eeze</u>
19. sug<u>gestion</u>
20. b<u>ite</u>

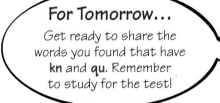

For Tomorrow...
Get ready to share the words you found that have **kn** and **qu**. Remember to study for the test!

Get Word Wise

The word *squirrel* comes from two Greek words: *skia*, meaning "shadow," and *oura*, meaning "tail." Together these words made the new word *skiouros*. The Greeks had noticed that when a squirrel sits up, it often raises its tail over its head as if to shade itself.

Word Study Strategy

See the word

START

Say it slowly

Link sounds and letters

Write

Check

END

Spellings for /z/

Ⓐ See and Say

Spelling Words

zoo	size
zipper	prize
zero	surprise
zebra	wise
lizard	freeze
buzz	sneeze
fuzzy	cheese
puzzle	tease
lazy	froze
crazy	chose

LOOKOUT WORD

Review	Challenge
quiet	xylophone
piece	disease
because	

My Words

The Spelling Concept

zero	puzzle	cheese
sneeze	buzz	wise

The letters z, zz, and s can stand for /z/.

A surprise will make your spirits rise.

MEMORY JOGGER

Ⓑ Link Sounds and Letters

Say each spelling word. Listen for /z/. Look at each word to find the letters that spell the sound. Then sort the words on a chart like this one.

Word Sort

z__	__z__	__zz	__zz__	__s__

Ⓒ Write and Check

Follow the directions in the Word Puzzle. Write the spelling word that completes the puzzle.

_____

Change the first two letters of your answer to *l*, and write another spelling word.

_____

WORD PUZZLE

Start with sneeze.
Change eeze to are.
Change sn to h.
Change re to zy.
Change h to cr.

A Build Vocabulary: Nouns and Adjectives

A noun names a person, place, or thing. An adjective describes or gives more information about a noun. For each clue write an adjective and a noun from the spelling words.

a slow-moving reptile	a __1__ __2__
a wild-looking fastener	a __3__ __4__
an unclear bee sound	a __5__ __6__
a smart cheddar	a __7__ __8__

B Word Study: Plural Nouns

Most plural nouns are formed by adding *s*. Add *s* to a spelling word to make it plural. Write the word to complete the sentence.

9. Our yearly Wildlife Carnival had many unexpected _____.

10. Fourth-graders dressed up like wild animals. They looked as if they came from a dozen different _____.

11. The costumes came in many colors, shapes, and _____.

12. The most unusual costumes would win _____.

13. My bird costume had fringe that tickled my nose. I let out a couple of _____, even though I didn't have a cold.

14. The two students who were dressed like black-and-white striped _____ tied for first prize.

15. They won jigsaw _____ that had many pieces.

C Write

Write two sentences or a rhyme. Use these spelling words.

chose   froze   zero   tease   freeze

_____

_____

_____

Spell Chat
Ask a friend to name words that rhyme with *prize* and to tell the letters that stand for /z/.

Be a Spelling Sleuth
Read labels on clothes, food, and other products. Look for words with /z/. Can you *zip* it, *squeeze* it, or *freeze* it? Keep a list of the words you find.

Spelling Words

zoo	size
zipper	prize
zero	surprise *LOOKOUT WORD*
zebra	wise
lizard	freeze
buzz	sneeze
fuzzy	cheese
puzzle	tease
lazy	froze
crazy	chose

Review	Challenge
quiet	xylophone
piece	disease
because	

My Words

_____

_____

_____

_____

Spelling Words

zoo	size
zipper	prize
zero	surprise
zebra	wise
lizard	freeze
buzz	sneeze
fuzzy	cheese
puzzle	tease
lazy	froze
crazy	chose

Review	Challenge
quiet	xylophone
piece	disease
because	

My Words

Quick Write

Use three spelling words in one or two sentences about a fantasy animal.

A **Write About an Animal**

You may wish to do this activity on a computer.

You're a reporter for a nature magazine. Your assignment is to write a short article about an animal. Choose an animal you know something about. Tell where it lives, what it eats, and what it does. Use three spelling words.

B **Proofread**

Here's Jesse's article. He made three spelling errors, one punctuation error, and one capitalization error. He also forgot to indent his paragraph. Correct his errors.

Tip

Remember to indent each paragraph.

A gecko is a small lizerd. It is quite an amazing animal. Some of the things it can do may surprize you. it catches insects with its long tongue. After eating, it licks its face and eyes clean. A gecko grows new skin and sheds its old skin regularly. If it loses a peice of tail, it's not a disaster That's because it can grow back a new one!

PROOFREADING MARKS

∧ Add
⊙ Add a period
ℓ Take out
⟳ Move
≡ Capital letter
/ Small letter
¶ Indent paragraph

Now proofread your paragraph. Check for spelling, punctuation, and capitalization errors. Make sure you indented your paragraph.

ⓐ Use the Dictionary: Definitions

When you look up a word in a dictionary, you'll find its definition, or meaning. Here are definitions for four spelling words. Write the word that goes with each definition. Use your Spelling Dictionary to check your answers.

_____ *noun* A reward for winning a game or contest.

_____ *noun* A toy or game that tests one's mental skills.

_____ *noun* A fastener for clothes consisting of interlocking metal or plastic teeth.

_____ *noun* A food made from the solid parts of milk.

_____ *noun* The measurement that tells how large or small something is.

ⓑ Test Yourself

Complete each spelling word with the letter or letters that stand for /z/. Write the spelling words.

1. surpri_e
2. _ipper
3. snee_e
4. pri_e
5. _oo
6. _ebra
7. la_y

8. bu_ _
9. free_e
10. fu_ _y
11. li_ard
12. cra_y
13. pu_ _le
14. wi_e

15. fro_e
16. si_e
17. _ero
18. cho_e
19. tea_e
20. chee_e

For Tomorrow...
Get ready to share the words with **/z/** you discovered, and remember to study for your test!

Word Study Strategy

START

See the word

Say it slowly

Link sounds and letters

Write

Check

END

Spelling Words

fact	office
faint	suffer
family	fluffy
favorite	waffles
fantastic	traffic
film	buffalo
after	dolphin
often *LOOKOUT WORD*	elephant
off	telephone
offer	photograph

Review	Challenge
surprise	nephew
fur	physical
fault	

My Words

Learn and Spell

Spellings for /f/

A See and Say

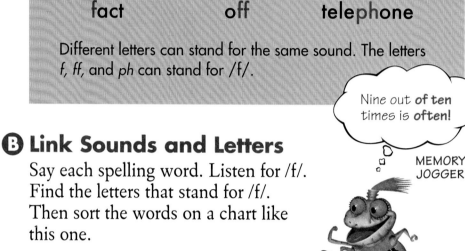

The Spelling Concept

fact   off   tele**ph**one

Different letters can stand for the same sound. The letters *f*, *ff*, and *ph* can stand for /f/.

Nine out of ten times is often!

MEMORY JOGGER

B Link Sounds and Letters

Say each spelling word. Listen for /f/. Find the letters that stand for /f/. Then sort the words on a chart like this one.

Word Sort

f__	__f__	__ff	__ff__	__ph__	ph__ph

C Write and Check

Read the riddle. Then write the spelling words that you find in it.

_____

_____

_____

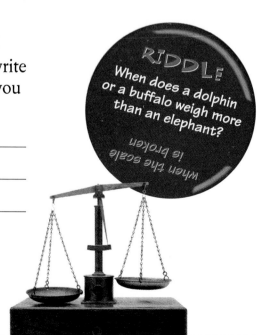

RIDDLE
When does a dolphin or a buffalo weigh more than an elephant?

When the scale is broken

Ⓐ Build Vocabulary: **Multiple Meanings**

Some words have more than one meaning. Read each pair of definitions. Then write the spelling words that go with them.

1. ■ to use a camera
   ■ a picture

2. ■ later than
   ■ follows behind

3. ■ not clear
   ■ dizzy or weak

4. ■ to call someone
   ■ a calling machine

5. ■ a breakfast food
   ■ changes one's mind

6. ■ a room in which to work
   ■ a job, such as mayor or president

Spell Chat
Pick a spelling word with two meanings. Challenge the person next to you to make up a sentence, using both meanings.

Ⓑ Word Study: **Analogies**

Write a spelling word to complete each analogy.

7. *Brick* is to *rough*, as *cotton* is to ___.
8. *Up* is to *down*, as *on* is to ___.
9. *Teacher* is to *class*, as *parent* is to ___.
10. *Arm* is to *farm*, as *act* is to ___ .
11. *Enjoy* is to *happy*, as ___ is to *sad*.
12. *Speak* is to *say*, as ___ is to *give*.
13. *Beak* is to *bird*, as *trunk* is to ___.
14. *Eagle* is to *sky*, as ___ is to *ocean*.
15. *Swamp* is to *alligator*, as *prairie* is to ___.
16. *Up* is to *down*, as ___ is to *seldom*.
17. *Best-liked is to* ___, as *funny* is to *amusing*.
18. *Tape* is to *cassette* player, as ___ is to *camera*.
19. *Wonderful* is to ___, as *terrible* is to *awful*.

Ⓒ Write

Write a sentence using **traffic** and **fault**.

_____

_____

Spelling Words

fact	office
faint	suffer
family	fluffy
favorite	waffles
fantastic	traffic
film	buffalo
after	dolphin
often	elephant
off	telephone
offer	photograph

Review	Challenge
surprise	nephew
fur	physical
fault	

My Words

_____

_____

_____

_____

Spelling Words

fact	office
faint	suffer
family	fluffy
favorite	waffles
fantastic	traffic
film	buffalo
after	dolphin
often LOOKOUT WORD	elephant
off	telephone
offer	photograph

Review	Challenge
surprise	nephew
fur	physical
fault	

My Words

_____

_____

_____

_____

Quick Write

Write three sentences about a surprising event. Use at least four of your spelling words.

You may wish to do this activity on a computer.

A Write a Paragraph

Imagine that you are eating in a restaurant when a person you admire walks in. Write a paragraph about what happens. Use at least three spelling words, and remember to write in complete sentences.

B Proofread

Here is Margaret's paragraph about meeting Dr. Shannon Lucid, the astronaut. Margaret made four spelling errors and one punctuation error. She also wrote one incomplete sentence. Correct the errors.

Tip
Make sure every sentence has a subject and a verb.

> Uncle Ralph and I were eating breakfast in a restaurant last week. To our surprize, Dr. Shannon Lucid, the astronaut, walked by. I thought I would faint!
>
> "Those wafles look fantastic," she said as she passed us. Uncle Ralph ran off to get fillm to fotograf us together. Was the best breakfast of my life

PROOFREADING MARKS

∧ Add
⊙ Add a period
ℓ Take out
↻ Move
≡ Capital letter
/ Small letter
¶ Indent paragraph

Now proofread your paragraph. Check for spelling, punctuation, and complete sentences.

Study and Review

A Use the Dictionary: Definitions

The dictionary lists the different meanings for a word and numbers them. Read the entry for *waffle*.

> **waf•fle** /wäf əl/
> 1. *noun* A type of cake baked in an appliance that presses a crisscross pattern into it. 2. *verb* To avoid giving a direct answer to a question; to keep changing your mind or position. *The politician waffled on the question of raising taxes.*

Read each sentence. Write the number for the meaning of *waffle*.

_____ Did your mom waffle about raising your allowance?

_____ I only want one waffle on my plate.

Write a sentence using *waffle* as a noun or a verb.

_____

B Test Yourself

Identify how /f/ is spelled in each word. Write the spelling words.

1. __ act	**8.** __ amily	**15.** bu __ __ alo
2. __ aint	**9.** a __ ter	**16.** dol __ __ in
3. o __ __ er	**10.** flu __ __ y	**17.** __ antastic
4. o __ ten	**11.** o __ __ ice	**18.** __ __ otogra __ __
5. su __ __ er	**12.** __ avorite	**19.** tele __ __ one
6. o __ __	**13.** wa __ __ les	**20.** ele __ __ ant
7. tra __ __ ic	**14.** __ ilm	

For Tomorrow...
Get ready to share the spelling for words with **/f/,** and remember to study for your test!

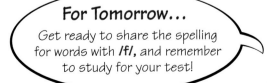

Get Word Wise
Did you know that when you take a *photograph*, you are writing on film with light? The word *photograph* is made up of two Greek words. *Photo* means "light." *Graph* means "I write."

Word Study Strategy

START

See the word

Say it slowly

Link sounds and letters

Write

Check

END

Learn and Spell

Words With mb

Ⓐ See and Say

Spelling Words

bumblebee	mumble
climb	numb
comb	number
crumb	remember
crumble	scramble
lamb	stumble
limb	thumb
limber	timber
lumber	tremble
member	tumble

LOOKOUT WORD

Review	Challenge
often	grumble
measles	jamboree
camp	

My Words

_____

_____

_____

The Spelling Concept

mb at the end	climb	comb
mb in the middle	number	tremble

When the letters *mb* are at the end of a word, they stand for /m/ as in *climb*. You don't hear /b/. When the letters *mb* are in the middle of a word, you hear both /m/ and /b/, as in *number*.

> You don't hear the hum of the **b** in **thumb**.

MEMORY JOGGER

Ⓑ Link Sounds and Letters

Say each spelling word. Listen–do you hear /b/? Then sort the words on a chart like this.

Word Sort	
Do you hear /b/?	
Yes	No

Ⓒ Write and Check

Read the joke. Then write the spelling words.

_____

_____

JOKE
What do you call a bumblebee with a low buzz?

a mumble bee

Vocabulary Practice

Ⓐ Build Vocabulary: Action Verbs

Read each sentence. Write a spelling word that means the same or almost the same thing as the underlined action verb or phrase.

1. <u>Loosen up</u>, and get ready for your camping trip.

2. Please <u>don't forget</u> to bring sunscreen and a hat.

3. You will have to <u>neaten</u> your hair, too.

4. For breakfast, we can <u>mix up</u> some eggs.

5. In the afternoon, we'll <u>hike up</u> a mountain.

6. Don't step on any rocks that can <u>break into pieces</u>.

7. Be careful not to <u>trip</u> over tree roots, either.

8. If you want to hear an echo, don't <u>speak too quietly</u>.

> **Spell Chat**
> Turn to the person next to you. Ask him or her to name two other spelling words that can be action verbs, and use them in a sentence.

Ⓑ Word Study: Word Clues

Write the spelling word that goes with each clue.

9. a tiny piece of bread
10. shake and shiver
11. a tree branch
12. turn a somersault
13. a baby sheep
14. a buzzing insect
15. rhymes with *number*
16. part of a group
17. a finger
18. a numeral
19. frozen
20. rhymes with *limber*

Ⓒ Write

Write a sentence, using the word *often*.

Be a Spelling Sleuth

Look through garden and nature magazines. Make a list of words with mb. For example, *bumblebee, cucumber, September.*

Spelling Words

bumblebee	mumble
climb	numb
comb	number
crumb	remember
crumble	scramble
lamb	stumble
limb	thumb
limber	timber
lumber	tremble
member	tumble

Review	Challenge
often	grumble
measles	jamboree
camp	

My Words

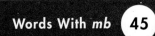

You may wish to do this activity on a computer.

Spelling Words

bumblebee	mumble
climb	numb
comb	number
crumb	remember
crumble	scramble
lamb	stumble
limb	thumb LOOKOUT WORD
limber	timber
lumber	tremble
member	tumble

Review	Challenge
often	grumble
measles	jamboree
camp	

My Words

Quick Write

Write a sentence that tells about something that happened at home or school. Then tell why it happened. Use at least three spelling words.

A Write a Cause/Effect Description

Imagine it's evening, and all the lights have suddenly gone out in your house. No one in the neighborhood has electricity. Write about what happens in your house. Use at least three spelling words.

B Proofread

Alex wrote this description. He made three spelling errors, one capitalization error, one punctuation error, and one error using an apostrophe. Correct them.

Tip
To make a singular noun possessive, add an apostrophe and s ('s). To make most plural nouns possessive, just add an apostrophe.

> It was Friday night. Every membr of my family was in the living room, playing a game. Suddenly, all the lights went out. Everything went black! my sister dog began to bark. I had to clime the stairs and stumble around in the dark to find my father's flashlight Then it began to get cold, so we decided to sleep in the living room by the wood stove. It was just like a kamp out.

PROOFREADING MARKS

∧ Add
⊙ Add a period
ℓ Take out
◠ Move
≡ Capital letter
/ Small letter
¶ Indent paragraph

Now proofread your description. Check spelling, capitalization, punctuation, and the correct use of apostrophes in possessive nouns.

A Use the Dictionary: Parts of Speech

What part of speech is a word? A dictionary entry tells you. It labels a word as a noun, verb, adjective, adverb, preposition, and so on. Some words can be more than one part of speech. Here is a dictionary entry for *comb*.

> **comb** /kōm/
> 1. *noun* A flat piece of metal or plastic with a row of teeth, used for making your hair smooth and neat.
> 2. *verb* To use a comb.
> 3. *verb* To search a place thoroughly.
> ▶ *verb* **combing, combed**

Read each sentence. Write *noun* or *verb* to tell which part of speech *comb* is.

She left her comb and brush in the hotel. _____

I combed my room trying to find my homework. _____

Write another sentence for the other meaning of *comb*.

_____

B Test Yourself

Reorder the syllables and letters to make spelling words. Look for letters that should go together, such as *mb*. Write each word.

1. berlum
2. bermem
3. bletum
4. blebumbee
5. bletrem
6. blemum
7. blescram
8. bertim
9. bernum
10. blecrum
11. berlim
12. blestum
13. memreber
14. umbth
15. bcrum
16. munb
17. clmib
18. obcm
19. blam
20. mlib

For Tomorrow...
Get ready to share the words with **mb** you found in garden and nature magazines. Remember to study for the test.

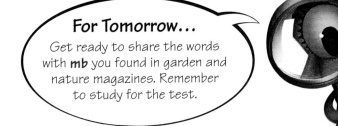

Get Word Wise

Is having a "green thumb" something to worry about? Not at all. This idiom describes someone who has a special talent for growing plants. When gardeners rub the leaves of some plants between their fingers, chlorophyll may rub off and turn their thumbs green.

Word Study Strategy

See the word — START — Say it slowly — Link sounds and letters — Write — Check — END

Spelling Words

able   noodle
apple   puddle
bottle   sample
bubble   simple
castle   sparkle
freckles   tickle
little   nickel
middle   twinkle
poodle   whistle
people   wiggle

Review	Challenge
thumb	pumpernickel
drowsy	squiggle
gentle	

My Words

_____

_____

_____

_____

Words With /əl/

A See and Say

The Spelling Concept

able   little   simple   nickel

The schwa sound is the sound you hear in an unaccented syllable. The /əl/ sound is often spelled *le*, but is sometimes spelled *el*.

> Toot, toot, toot ... Don't forget the **t** in whis**t**le!

MEMORY JOGGER

B Link Sounds and Letters

Say each spelling word. Listen for /əl/. Look at the letters that spell /əl/. Sort the words on a chart like this one.

Word Sort

one consonant before /əl/	two different consonants before /əl/	double consonants before /əl/

C Write and Check

Find the spelling words in the rhyme. Then use two other spelling words to write a sentence or a rhyme.

_____

_____

RHYME
I didn't eat the noodle,
So I gave it to my poodle.

A Build Vocabulary: **Related Words**

Write the spelling word that goes with the other words
in each group.

1. jiggle, squirm, _____
2. please, amuse, _____
3. palace, mansion, _____
4. sparkle, shimmer, _____
5. pasta, macaroni, _____
6. easy, clear, _____
7. center, halfway, _____
8. folks, persons, _____

Spell Chat

Challenge a classmate to
think of two more words that
end with /əl/ and rhyme with
spelling words. How is /əl/
spelled in those words?

B Word Study: **Plurals**

To make most words plural, you add *s*,
as in *riddles*. Write the plurals of spelling
words to complete these sentences.

9. Our new puppies are miniature ___.
10. We feed them milk from ___, just
    like babies.
11. One puppy has lots of brown ___
    on his nose.
12. They love to splash in muddy ___ after it rains.
13. They play with the red ___ that fell from our tree.
14. We blow soap ___ for them to chase.
15. Sometimes we give them small ___ of our food.
16. We are saving our ___, dimes, and quarters to buy
    them toys.
17. We are training them to come when we blow our ___.

C Write

Write directions for decorating an eye-catching poster
with glitter. Use these spelling words.

able	little	sparkle

_____

_____

Be a Spelling Sleuth

Look for /əl/ words about toys
and games in stores, catalogs, and
magazine ads. For example, *castles*,
whistles, *easels*, and
bicycle. Keep a list
of words.

Spelling Words

able	poodle
apple	puddle
bottle	sample
bubble	simple
castle	sparkle
freckles	tickle
little	nickel
middle	twinkle
noodle	whistle
people	wiggle

Review	Challenge
thumb	pumpernickel
drowsy	squiggle
gentle	

My Words

_____

_____

_____

_____

You may wish to do this activity on a computer.

Spelling Words

able	noodle
apple	puddle
bottle	sample
bubble	simple
castle	sparkle
freckles	tickle
little	nickel
middle	twinkle
poodle	whistle
people	wiggle

LOOKOUT WORD

Review	Challenge
thumb	pumpernickel
drowsy	squiggle
gentle	

My Words

_____

_____

_____

_____

Quick Write

Write a headline for a news article. Include at least three spelling words.

A Write a Weather Report

Imagine you are the most popular weather reporter in your city. Write your forecast. Make it colorful. Use at least four spelling words.

B Proofread

Blanca wrote this weather report. She made four spelling errors and one capitalization error. She also forgot to use an exclamation point where one was needed. Correct the errors.

Tip

Use an exclamation mark at the end of an exclamatory word, phrase, or sentence.

It's going to be a perfect day here in miami. The sun will make the water sparkle. Gentel winds will tikle the palm trees. In the middle of the day, we may see a few littel clouds. So wiggle into your bathing suit early, grab a botel of ice-cold water, and head for the beach. Wow, what a day

PROOFREADING MARKS

∧ Add
⊙ Add a period
ℓ Take out
⌒∧ Move
≡ Capital letter
/ Small letter
¶ Indent paragraph

Now proofread your paragraph. Check for spelling, punctuation, and capitalization.

A Use the Dictionary: **Word Endings**

How do you spell a word that has an ending added?
Just look up the base word in the dictionary. Here is the
entry for the base word *bubble*.

> **bub•ble** /bub əl/
> 1. *noun* One of the tiny balls of gas in fizzy drinks, boiling
> water, and so on. 2. *verb* To make bubbles. *The boiling
> water bubbled.* ▸ *verb* **bubbling, bubbled**

Write *bubble* with the endings shown in the entry.

_____   _____

Write the base word you would look up in the dictionary to
find each of these words.

sampled _____   wiggling _____

whistling _____   tickled _____

B Test Yourself

Write the spelling words from the letter clues given below.

1. _ eo _ _ _ _	**8.** p _ dd _ _	**15.** b _ bb _ _
2. n _ ck _ _	**9.** c _ st _ _	**16.** l _ tt _ _
3. ab _ _	**10.** sp _ rk _ _	**17.** n _ _ d _ _
4. w _ is _ _ _	**11.** p _ _ d _ _	**18.** t _ ck _ _
5. m _ dd _ _	**12.** fr _ _ k _ _s	**19.** tw _ nk _ _
6. b _ tt _ _	**13.** a _ _ _ _	**20.** w _ gg _ _
7. _ am _ _ _	**14.** _ im _ _ _	

> ### For Tomorrow...
> Get ready to share your /əl/
> words about toys and games.
> Remember to study for your test!

Word Study Strategy

See the word

START

Say it slowly

Link sounds and letters

Write

Check

END

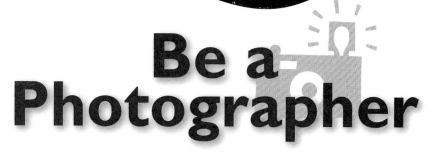

Be a Photographer

Complete each sentence with a spelling word from the box.

question	surprise	favorite
often	photograph	people

My name is Shelby Blake, and I'm a photographer. I like to (1) animals. They are my (2) subjects. When I show my pictures to (3) , they (4) ask me, "How do you get such natural-looking pictures of animals?" My answer to that (5) may (6) you.

squirrel	crazy	fantastic
limb	climb	scramble

If you want to take good pictures of animals, you have to wait for them. I once had to (7) a tree and (8) out onto a (9) . I wanted to get a picture of a gray (10) . I stayed up in the tree for almost an hour. I felt a little (11) , but I got a (12) picture.

sneeze	buffalo	remember
tickle	froze	whistle

Another trick I use when I photograph animals is to (13) a tune softly. An animal will usually look up to see from where the sound is coming. However, I (14) one time when I made a noise that ruined my picture. I was trying to photograph a (15) and her calf. Things were going well until I felt this (16) in my nose. I couldn't do anything to stop the loud (17) that followed. The animals (18) for a moment. Then they took off in a cloud of dust.

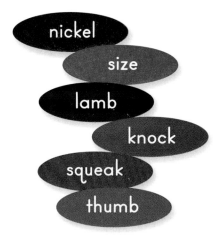

nickel

size

lamb

knock

squeak

thumb

Rhyming Words

Write the spelling words that rhyme with the words below. Remember, words that rhyme do not always have the same ending letters.

1. hum, some, _____

2. rock, flock, _____

3. ties, buys, _____

4. pickle, tickle, _____

5. cheek, week, _____

6. jam, clam, _____

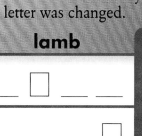

Word Ladder

Go from *lamb* to *tame*. Change just one letter at a time to make a new word. The box shows you which letter was changed.

lamb

___ ___ □ ___

___ ___ ___ □

□ ___ ___ ___

tame

Synonyms and Antonyms

wise	little	off	after	simple
quiet	faint	fantastic	quick	offer

Write the spelling word that is a synonym and an antonym for the words below.

Synonym   **Antonym**

7. fast _____ slow

8. easy _____ hard

9. smart _____ foolish

10. small _____ large

11. shut down _____ on

12. wonderful _____ awful

13. peaceful _____ noisy

14. give _____ take

15. behind _____ before

16. weak _____ strong

Lesson 12 Review

knight   people

know   elephant

queen   telephone

lizard   quiet

puzzle   stumble

froze   surprise

favorite   remember

middle

Tip

Make sure you include all the letters in words that have silent letters.

PROOFREADING MARKS

∧ Add
⊙ Add a period
ℓ Take out
↻∧ Move
≡ Capital letter
/ Small letter
¶ Indent paragraph

What's Next?

The beginning of a story lets you know what the story is about. Read each story starter. Then write the next sentence. Use at least two spelling words in each sentence.

1. The castle on the hill looked deserted.

_____

_____

2. Last summer I went to Africa with my Aunt Tanya.

_____

_____

3. Did you ever hear about the winter when polar bears wore overcoats?

_____

_____

4. Detective Johnson heard something ringing.

_____

_____

5. Jill wondered if anyone remembered her birthday.

_____

_____

Look back at My Words and the words you misspelled in your Unit 2 Posttests. Use them to write the next sentence for this story starter.

6. The spacecraft landed on a faraway planet.

_____

_____

Write It

Write the first paragraph of a short story, using one of the sentence pairs from above. Proofread for spelling, capitalization, and punctuation. Then read it to a friend.

Unusual Combinations

Many words have unusual letter combinations, such as *kn*, *qu*, *zz*, *ph*, and *mb*. Such words can be tricky because they often have silent letters or surprising sounds.

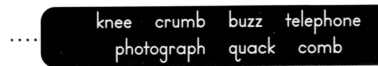

.... knee crumb buzz telephone
photograph quack comb ....

Write the spelling word that completes each phrase.

1. kittens meow, bees _____

2. arm and elbow, leg and _____

3. type and computer, talk and _____

4. _____ your hair, tie your shoe

5. birds chirp, ducks _____

6. phone and telephone, photo and _____

7. ice cube, bread _____

.... knife square squeak question
mumble remember scramble puzzle ....

Write a spelling word for each clue. Then write the boxed letters in order to answer the riddle.

8. not speak clearly ☐ _ _ _ _ _ _

9. a shape that has four equal sides _ _ ☐ _ _ _

10. the opposite of *forget* _ _ ☐ _ ☐ _ _

11. something to be figured out _ _ _ _ ☐ _

12. something that needs an answer _ _ ☐ _ _ _ _

13. one way to cook eggs _ _ _ _ ☐ _ _

14. the sound a mouse makes _ _ _ ☐ _ _

15. use this to cut an apple _ _ _ _ ☐

RIDDLE
What is a bee with a low buzz?

a _ _ _ _ _ _ _
_ _ _ _

Words With /ər/

A See and Say

The Spelling Concept

| /ər/ | winter | cellar | flavor |

The schwa sound, /ə/, is the sound you hear in an unaccented syllable. The /ər/ sound is often spelled *er* as in *winter*. It can also be spelled *ar* and *or*.

The drawing of Erna is in the drawer.

MEMORY JOGGER

B Link Sounds and Letters

Say each spelling word. Listen for the ending /ər/. Sort the words on a chart like this one.

Word Sort

/ər/ spelled er	/ər/ spelled ar	/ər/ spelled or	Other Words

C Write and Check

Which words end in /ər/? Write the three that are spelling words.

_____

_____

_____

Spelling Words

calendar
caterpillar
cellar
chapter
chatter
checkers
collar
cracker
deliver
dollar

drawer — LOOKOUT WORD
elevator
flavor
hamburger
harbor
horror
scatter
seller
summer
winter

Review	Challenge
nickel	professor
cough	similar
color	

My Words

_____

_____

_____

RIDDLE

Why do cats sleep better in the summer than in the winter?

(because summer brings the caterpillar (the cat is a pillow))

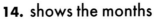

A Build Vocabulary: **Word Meaning**

Write the spelling word that goes with each clue.

1. port
2. basement
3. trader
4. four quarters
5. not winter
6. coldest season
7. part of a dresser
8. part of a book
9. biscuit
10. neckband
11. lifts you up
12. great fear
13. board game
14. shows the months
15. a sandwich
16. becomes a butterfly

Spell Chat

Challenge a classmate to think of three more words that end with **/ər/**, and make up word clues for them.

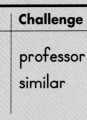

B Word Study: **Past-Tense Verbs**

Most past-tense verbs end in -ed. Read the word in parentheses, and write the past-tense verb that completes each sentence.

17. (chatter) The class ——— excitedly about the pizza party.

18. (deliver) At noon, Smiling Pizza ——— five large pies.

19. (scatter) Vegetables were ——— on top of one pizza.

20. (flavor) The sauce was ——— with herbs and spices.

C Write

Imagine that you are writing a book. Write the book's title and the title of the first chapter. Use three spelling words.

_____

_____

Be a Spelling Sleuth

Look in your school for signs and labels with two-syllable words ending in /ər/. For example, *Water Fountain, Teacher's Lounge.* Keep a list.

Spelling Words

calendar	drawer
caterpillar	elevator
cellar	flavor
chapter	hamburger
chatter	harbor
checkers	horror
collar	scatter
cracker	seller
deliver	summer
dollar	winter

Review	Challenge
nickel	professor
cough	similar
color	

My Words

_____

_____

_____

_____

You may wish to do this activity on a computer.

Spelling Words

calendar	drawer
caterpillar	elevator
cellar	flavor
chapter	hamburger
chatter	harbor
checkers	horror
collar	scatter
cracker	seller
deliver	summer
dollar	winter

Review	Challenge
nickel	professor
cough	similar
color	

My Words

_____

_____

_____

_____

Quick Write

Write a short e-mail message to a friend about something that happened last weekend. Use at least three spelling words.

A Write a Personal Narrative

What was the last celebration you shared with friends or family? What was the season? Write a paragraph describing the celebration. Use at least four spelling words in your personal narrative.

B Proofread

Risa wrote a personal narrative to put in her scrapbook. She made four spelling errors, one capitalization error, and one punctuation error. Help her correct her errors.

Tip
A sentence begins with a capital letter. Use a question mark at the end of a question and a period after a statement.

today we celebrated the end of the summer with a picnic at the harbor. Everyone ate a hot dog or hamberger. There were lots of games and prizes, too. I entered a race for a nickle and won a dollar! I also received a game of checkers when I won the ring toss. I guess the prizes will come in handy this wintr when I'm playing indoors with my little sister

PROOFREADING MARKS

∧ Add
⊙ Add a period
ℓ Take out
↶↷ Move
≡ Capital letter
/ Small letter
¶ Indent paragraph

Now proofread your personal narrative. Check your spelling, capitalization, and punctuation.

Ⓐ Use the Dictionary: Syllables

An entry word is separated into syllables. A syllable is a word part that has a vowel sound. Most dictionaries separate syllables with a dot. Here is the entry word *chatter*.

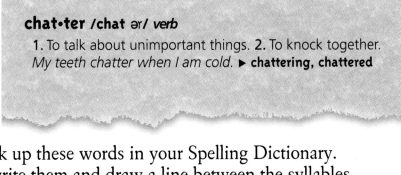

chat•ter /chat ər/ *verb*
1. To talk about unimportant things. 2. To knock together. *My teeth chatter when I am cold.* ▶ **chattering, chattered**

Look up these words in your Spelling Dictionary. Rewrite them and draw a line between the syllables.

dollar _____   cellar _____

hamburger _____   deliver _____

harbor _____   calendar _____

Ⓑ Test Yourself

Add one or more syllables to make a spelling word. Write the complete word. Remember that the Lookout Word has only one syllable.

1. fla__   8. cal____   15. win__
2. check__   9. cel__   16. sell__
3. ham____   10. chat__   17. dol__
4. har__   11. chap__   18. sum__
5. crack__   12. el____   19. scat__
6. col__   13. de____   20. __
7. cat____   14. hor__

For Tomorrow...
Get ready to share the /ər/ words you've discovered, and remember to study for your test!

Word Study Strategy

START
See the word
Say it slowly
Link sounds and letters
Write
Check
END

Spelling Words

basket	fossil *LOOKOUT WORD*
better	happen
blizzard	letter
borrow	mirror
bottom	pattern
button	pepper
cotton	pillow
dinner	puppet
fellow	silver
follow	supper

Review	Challenge
drawer	stirrup
squirrel	gossip
kitten	

My Words

Syllable Pattern: VCCV

A See and Say

The Spelling Concept

	VC	CV
basket	bas	ket
dinner	din	ner

In a two-syllable word, each syllable has a vowel sound. When the first syllable has a short vowel sound, the spelling pattern is VCCV, vowel-consonant-consonant-vowel.

I see an i in fossil.

MEMORY JOGGER

B Link Sounds and Letters

Say each spelling word. Listen to the vowel sound in the first syllable. Sort the words. Underline the two consonants that follow the first vowel.

Word Sort

/a/	/e/	/i/	/o/	/u/

C Write and Check

Which words in the riddle have the VCCV pattern? Write the two that are spelling words.

RIDDLE

Why did the fellow sprinkle chili pepper on his car's tires?

He wanted a set of hot wheels.

_____

_____

A Build Vocabulary: Adjectives

Adjectives are words that describe nouns. Read each sentence. Write the adjective that is a spelling word.

1. Everyone helped hang the blue and silver streamers for the school celebration.

2. All the students wore the cotton T-shirts that they had tie-dyed.

3. Michelle eagerly waited on the bottom step for the rest of her class.

4. She knew that there wouldn't be a better day in the entire school year.

Spell Chat
Name a noun, and ask a classmate to think of an adjective to describe it. Use one of the spelling words.

B Word Study: Categories

Write the spelling word that fits in each group. Note that two spelling words fit in the last item.

5. man, boy, ——

6. snow, storm, ——

7. mattress, blanket, ——

8. note, memo, ——

9. rock, shell, ——

10. box, container, ——

11. doll, toy, ——

12. design, model, ——

13. salt, chili powder, ——

14. zipper, snap, ——

15. go after, trail, ——

16. occur, take place, ——

17–18. breakfast, lunch, ——, ——

C Write

Write a sentence using these spelling words.

borrow   mirror

_____

_____

Spelling Words

basket	fossil *LOOKOUT WORD*
better	happen
blizzard	letter
borrow	mirror
bottom	pattern
button	pepper
cotton	pillow
dinner	puppet
fellow	silver
follow	supper

Review	Challenge
drawer	stirrup
squirrel	gossip
kitten	

My Words

_____

_____

_____

_____

You may wish to do this activity on a computer.

Spelling Words

basket	fossil
better	happen
blizzard	letter
borrow	mirror
bottom	pattern
button	pepper
cotton	pillow
dinner	puppet
fellow	silver
follow	supper

Review	Challenge
drawer	stirrup
squirrel	gossip
kitten	

My Words

Quick Write

Use as many spelling words as you can in a sentence describing a scene in a puppet show.

A Write About a Setting

Imagine that you and your classmates are writing a play. Write a setting for the play. Describe the time and place in which the action of the play happens. Use three spelling words.

B Proofread

Ken described the setting for his class play. In his description, Ken made three spelling errors, one error in capitalization, and forgot one apostrophe in a possessive noun. Correct the errors.

Tip

Add an apostrophe after the s of a plural noun to make it possessive.

> The play "Summer Blizard" is set in the Rocky Mountains of colorado. Everything seems perfect as families arrive for their summer vacations. The silver lake looks as smooth as a mirrer. White clouds dot the sky like puffs of cotton. The trees leaves are bright green. A squirel sits on a branch. In the distance, snow covers the mountains. Something unusual is about to happen.

PROOFREADING MARKS

∧ Add
⊙ Add a period
ℓ Take out
↶↷ Move
≡ Capital letter
／ Small letter
¶ Indent paragraph

Now proofread your setting. Check for spelling, capitalization, and punctuation. Make sure you add an apostrophe to possessive nouns.

A Use the Dictionary: Stressed Syllables

A dictionary entry tells you how to pronounce a word. Some dictionaries show the accented syllable in dark letters. Other dictionaries use an accent mark to show which syllable is stressed. Here are two ways to show how *basket* is pronounced.

/**bas** kit/   /bas′ kit/

The spelling words below are divided into syllables. Say each word, and listen for the accented syllable. Then write the word, and underline the accented syllable. Check your answers in the Spelling Dictionary.

pup pet _____   bliz zard _____

sil ver _____   mir ror _____

sup per _____   let ter _____

din ner _____   fol low _____

B Test Yourself

Rearrange the syllables, and write the spelling word.

1. ton but
2. low fel
3. per pep
4. sil fos
5. pet pup
6. low pil
7. ket bas
8. per sup
9. pen hap
10. ter bet
11. tom bot
12. ver sil
13. zard bliz
14. tern pat
15. ter let
16. row bor
17. ton cot
18. ner din
19. low fol
20. ror mir

For Tomorrow...
Get ready to share the **VCCV** words you discovered, and remember to study for the test!

Get Word Wise

The word *fossil* comes from the Latin word *fossilis*, meaning "dug up." The remains of ancient animals and plants are usually covered with rock or buried deep in the ground. Now you can see how fossils got their name.

Word Study Strategy

See the word

START

Say it slowly

Link sounds and letters

Write

Check

END

LESSON 15

Spelling Words

diner	paper
even	pilot
favor	pirate *LOOKOUT WORD*
fever	radio
final	silent
hotel	spider
moment	super
open	tiger
over	tiny
notice	tuna

Review	Challenge
fossil	spiral
crazy	laser
music	

My Words

Syllable Pattern: VCV

Ⓐ See and Say

The Spelling Concept

VCV

favor   fa vor

In a two-syllable word, each syllable has a vowel sound. When the first syllable has a long vowel sound, the spelling pattern is VCV. VCV stands for vowel-consonant-vowel.

> One n for a diner, and two for a dinner.

MEMORY JOGGER

Ⓑ Link Sounds and Letters

Say each spelling word. Listen to the vowel sound in the first syllable. Sort the words. Underline the consonant that follows the first vowel.

Word Sort

/ā/	/ē/	/ī/	/ō/	/o͞o/

Ⓒ Write and Check

Which words in the tongue twister have a long vowel sound followed by a single consonant letter? Write the three spelling words.

TONGUE TWISTER
The silent spider spins a super web in a spectacular spot.

_____

_____

_____

A Build Vocabulary: **Word Meaning**

Write the spelling word that fits in each clue.

1. ___ station
2. sore throat and ___
3. last or ___
4. inn or ___
5. wait a ___
6. to see or ___
7. a ___ fish sandwich
8. a ___ and its cubs
9. do someone a ___
10. a ___ with eight legs
11. wonderful or ___
12. a ___ treasure chest
13. eat in a ___
14. a ___ flying an airplane
15. a sheet of ___

B Word Study: **Opposites**

Words such as *heavy* and *light* are opposites.
Write the spelling word that is the opposite
of each word.

16. not huge, but ___
17. not closed, but ___
18. not under, but ___
19. not noisy, but ___
20. not odd, but ___

C Write

Write a notice for the school newspaper announcing a
super upcoming event. Use at least three spelling words.

_____

_____

_____

Be a Spelling Sleuth

Look at signs for two-syllable words
with the VCV spelling
pattern; for
example, *Hotel
Open* or *Super Sale.*
Keep a list.

Spell Chat
Give a classmate a clue
for a word with the *VCV* pattern.
Ask the classmate to name
the word that fits the clue,
and to identify the
first vowel sound.

Spelling Words

diner	paper
even	pilot
favor	pirate *LOOKOUT WORD*
fever	radio
final	silent
hotel	spider
moment	super
open	tiger
over	tiny
notice	tuna

Review	Challenge
fossil	spiral
crazy	laser
music	

My Words

_____

_____

_____

_____

You may wish to do this activity on a computer.

Spelling Words

diner	paper
even	pilot
favor	pirate
fever	radio
final	silent
hotel	spider
moment	super
open	tiger
over	tiny
notice	tuna

Review	Challenge
fossil	spiral
crazy	laser
music	

My Words

_____

_____

_____

_____

Quick Write

Write three sentences about someone in your family or a friend. Tell what is special about the person. Use at least three spelling words.

Ⓐ Write Interview Questions

Imagine that you are going to write a biographical sketch of someone you know or admire. What kind of information would you want to find out? Write four questions you would ask. Use four spelling words.

Ⓑ Proofread

Mark wrote four questions he would ask a firefighter. He made three spelling errors, one punctuation error, and two errors in subject-verb agreement. Correct the errors.

Tip

Identify the subject of the sentence. Then check to make sure the subject and verb agree.

1. How did you becomes a supper firefighter?
2. What do you do the momment the fire alarm rings at the fire station?
3. When you are not fighting a fire, does you enjoy sports, muzic, or other hobbies?
4. What do you like most about your job

PROOFREADING MARKS

∧ Add
⊙ Add a period
ℓ Take out
↶↗ Move
≡ Capital letter
/ Small letter
¶ Indent paragraph

Now proofread your interview questions. Check your spelling, punctuation, and subject-verb agreement.

Ⓐ Use the Dictionary: Pronunciation Key

Dictionary entries show you how to pronounce a word. The word is written with the letters and symbols found in the pronunciation key. Here is part of a pronunciation key and entry for *paper*.

pa·per /pā̇ pər/ *noun*

ā **a**ce	ə = in **a**bove
ē **e**qual	ə = in sick**e**n
ī **i**ce	ə = in poss**i**ble
ō **o**pen	ə = in mel**o**n
	ə = in circ**u**s

Use the pronunciation key to help you say each spelling word. The accented syllable is in darker type. Write the word.

/**fā** vər/ _____   /**ē** vən/ _____

/**tī** gər/ _____   /**hō** tel/ _____

Ⓑ Test Yourself

Figure out the missing syllables, and write spelling words.

1. fe ___
2. ___ment
3. ___pen
4. ___tel
5. din___
6. ___ven
7. ___rate
8. ___lot
9. spi___
10. ___ny
11. ___na
12. ___dio
13. pa___
14. ___vor
15. ___ver
16. no___
17. ___nal
18. ___ger
19. su___
20. ___lent

For Tomorrow…
Get ready to share the **VCV** words you found on signs, and be sure to study for your test!

Get Word Wise

Believe it or not, *dinner* meant "breakfast" in Middle English. Both *diner* and *dinner* come from the Latin word *disiunare*, meaning "to eat the first meal." In Middle English, *dinner* came to mean "the first big meal of the day," which was usually eaten in the morning. Now, most people eat their biggest meal at night!

Word Study Strategy

See the word

START

Say it slowly

Link sounds and letters

Write

Check

END

Words That End With ure

A See and Say

Spelling Words

measure   structure

pleasure   creature

treasure   feature

fracture   mixture

future   moisture   LOOKOUT WORD

nature   furniture

capture   adventure

pasture   literature

culture   temperature

picture   injure

Review	Challenge
pirate	gesture
favorite	pressure
turtle	

My Words

_____

_____

_____

_____

The Spelling Concept

measure   creature   injure

In an unaccented syllable, /ər/ can be spelled with the letters *ure*.

> When it's **moist**, there is **moisture**.

MEMORY JOGGER

B Link Sounds and Letters

Say each spelling word. Listen for the ending sounds in the word. Write the words in the correct column.

Word Sort

/zhər/	/chər/	/jər/

C Write and Check

Follow the directions in the Word Puzzle. Write the three spelling words you made.

_____

_____

_____

WORD PUZZLE

Think of a synonym for *hat*. Add *ture*.
Think of a synonym for *stir*. Add *ture*.
Think of a synonym for *wet*. Add *ure*.

A Build Vocabulary: Synonyms

Synonyms are words that have the same or nearly the same meaning. Write the spelling word that is a synonym for each of these words or phrases.

1. riches
2. tomorrow
3. a photo
4. to catch
5. to break
6. an exciting time
7. to hurt
8. a building
9. an animal
10. a field
11. outdoors
12. customs and traditions

Spell Chat

Challenge a classmate to think of at least two more synonyms for *treasure* and for *picture*. Remember, these words can be nouns or verbs.

B Word Study: Forming Words

When you add *ure* or *ture* to certain base words, they become nouns. The spelling of the base word may change slightly. Look at these words. Which spelling word can be formed by adding *ure* or *ture*? Write the spelling word.

13. mix
14. moist
15. please
16. furnish
17. literate
18. temperate

C Write

Write directions for making a parade costume.
Use these words:

feature   measure   favorite

_____

_____

_____

Be a Spelling Sleuth

Look in magazines and newspapers for words ending in ure. Can you find today's *temperature* or a *picture* puzzle? Keep a list.

Spelling Words

measure	structure
pleasure	creature
treasure	feature
fracture	mixture
future	moisture *LOOKOUT WORD*
nature	furniture
capture	adventure
pasture	literature
culture	temperature
picture	injure

Review	Challenge
pirate	gesture
favorite	pressure
turtle	

My Words

_____

_____

_____

_____

Spelling Words

measure	structure
pleasure	creature
treasure	feature
fracture	mixture
future	moisture LOOKOUT WORD
nature	furniture
capture	adventure
pasture	literature
culture	temperature
picture	injure

Review	Challenge
pirate	gesture
favorite	pressure
turtle	

My Words

Quick Write

You are a movie reviewer. Write a positive statement that will appear in an ad for a new science fiction movie. Use at least three spelling words.

You may wish to do this activity on a computer.

Ⓐ Write a Story Summary

Write a summary of a science fiction story about an undersea colony in the year 3000. Think about who the main character is. Figure out what happens. In your writing, remember to use object pronouns such as *me*, *you*, *him*, *her*, *it*, *us*, and *them* when you need them.

Ⓑ Proofread

Sonya wrote a brief summary of her science fiction story. She made four spelling errors and capitalized a letter that should have been small. She also used a noun where she could have used an object pronoun. Correct Sonya's errors.

Tip
For variety in your writing, use pronouns instead of repeating a word.

Zola, a twelve year old, lives in Aquia, an underwater City. She loves Aquia. One day she finds a pitcher of a land above the sea. It shows a green pasture and a furry creeture with horns. Zola decides to travel to this strange new place. With Oro, her faverite friend, she sets out on a hair-raising advencher.

PROOFREADING MARKS

∧ Add
⊙ Add a period
℮ Take out
ᴖ Move
≡ Capital letter
/ Small letter
¶ Indent paragraph

Now proofread your paragraph. Check spelling, capitalization, and the correct use of object pronouns.

Ⓐ Use the Dictionary: Parts of Speech

A dictionary entry has labels that tell which parts of speech a word can be. Some words can be more than one part of speech. Read the dictionary entry for *picture*.

> **pic•ture** /pik chər/
> 1. **noun** An image of something, such as a painting, photograph, or drawing. 2. **verb** To imagine something.

Read each sentence. Write whether the word *picture* is used as a noun or a verb.

_____ Gil took a picture of Jean riding a horse.

_____ Can you picture her wearing a cowboy hat?

Write a sentence in which *picture* is a verb.

_____

Ⓑ Test Yourself

Write the spelling word that goes with the clue.

1. a grassy _____
2. a tape _____
3. buried _____
4. smiles with _____
5. a furry _____
6. a _____ such as a nose
7. living room _____
8. draw a _____
9. a hot _____
10. a _____ of colors

11. to catch or _____
12. to break or _____
13. past, present, _____
14. customs of my _____
15. read good _____
16. an exciting _____
17. damp from _____
18. to hurt or _____
19. the world of _____
20. the _____ of the house

For Tomorrow...
Get ready to share the words with **ure** you discovered, and remember to study for the test.

Get Word Wise

The word *treasure* comes from the Greek word *thesauros* which means "something put away." Long ago people put away or stored a variety of things. Over the ages it came to mean wealth and riches. Today a treasure can be more than lots of money. It's also something that is loved and highly valued.

Word Study Strategy

See the word

START

Say it slowly

Link sounds and letters

Write

Check

END

Words With /ən/

Spelling Words

organ	reason
orphan	lemon
sudden	wagon
robin	lion
cabin	ocean
muffin	pigeon
cousin	captain
lesson	certain
ribbon	fountain
person	mountain

LOOKOUT WORD

Review	Challenge
moisture	loosen
crumble	lighten
garden	

My Words

_____

_____

_____

_____

Ⓐ See and Say

The Spelling Concept

organ   sudden   robin   lesson   certain

The schwa sound is the sound you hear in an unaccented syllable. The /ən/ is often spelled *on* as in *lesson*. It can also be spelled *an*, *en*, *in*, or *ain*.

Leon saw a pigeon.

MEMORY JOGGER

Ⓑ Link Sounds and Letters

Say each spelling word. Listen for /ən/. Look at each word to see how /ən/ is spelled. Then sort the words on a web like this one.

Word Sort

in

en

/ən/

on   an   ain

Ⓒ Write and Check

Read the riddle and find the words that end in /ən/. Then write an amusing sentence or a riddle. Use at least two spelling words.

RIDDLE

What would you get if you crossed a lion with a lemon?

a sourpuss that roars

_____

_____

Ⓐ Build Vocabulary: Nouns

A noun names a person, place, or thing. Which of your spelling words are nouns? Write the one that best completes each sentence.

Everyone was excited about the photo safari. We sailed across the __1__ to Africa. When the ship's __2__ announced that the ship was about to dock, we all cheered.

In port, the heat of the day hit us. I looked for a drinking __3__. The __4__ next to me began fanning herself with a magazine. Soon, however, we had a __5__ to forget about the heat. In the distance we could see Mount Cameroon, the highest __6__ in western Africa. It was beautiful.

Before long we were traveling in a station __7__ to a remote area. We caught a glimpse of a __8__ and its cubs in the grasslands. Out came the cameras. Our photo safari had begun.

Spell Chat

Challenge a classmate to say a sentence that has two nouns ending with /ən/. You identify the nouns.

Ⓑ Word Study: Word Meaning

Write the spelling word that answers each question.

9. What is a small house in the woods called?
10. What red-breasted bird is known as a sign of spring?
11. What word names a city bird that coos?
12. What word names a musical instrument like a piano?
13. What do you call your uncle's son or daughter?
14. What is a small bread that looks like a cupcake?
15. What is used to tie a package and to make a bow?
16. What yellow fruit is used to make a refreshing drink?
17. What is a name for a person without parents?
18. What word means "happening all at once"?
19. What word means "sure to happen"?
20. What is an experience that teaches you something?

Be a Spelling Sleuth

Look at picture books and fiction and nonfiction titles in a bookstore or library for words ending in /ən/. For example, *My Side of the Mountain* and *Give a Moose a Muffin*. Keep a list.

Spelling Words

organ	reason
orphan	lemon
sudden	wagon
robin	lion
cabin	ocean
muffin	pigeon LOOKOUT WORD
cousin	captain
lesson	certain
ribbon	fountain
person	mountain

Review	Challenge
moisture	loosen
crumble	lighten
garden	

My Words

_____

_____

_____

_____

You may wish to do this activity on a computer.

Spelling Words

organ	reason
orphan	lemon
sudden	wagon
robin	lion
cabin	ocean
muffin	pigeon *LOOKOUT WORD*
cousin	captain
lesson	certain
ribbon	fountain
person	mountain

Review	Challenge
moisture	loosen
crumble	lighten
garden	

My Words

Ⓐ Write a Persuasive Paragraph

You think that your town's new community center needs activities for young people. Write a letter to the mayor. Tell him or her which activities you would like and why. Persuade your mayor to take action! Use three spelling words in your letter.

Ⓑ Proofread

Ivan wrote this persuasive paragraph in his letter to the mayor. In his first draft, Ivan made four spelling errors, one capitalization error, and wrote one incomplete sentence. Correct the errors.

Tip
When you write, make sure each sentence has a subject and predicate.

> We need more programs for school children. the reasen is simple. Young people like me and my couson Jo have nothing to do on weekends. Would like to take swimming lessons, play sports, and plant a gardin. We know that you care about what happens to us. As mayor, you are the one persin who can help!

PROOFREADING MARKS

∧	Add
⊙	Add a period
ℓ	Take out
◯↗	Move
≡	Capital letter
/	Small letter
¶	Indent paragraph

Now proofread your persuasive paragraph. Check spelling and capitalization, and make sure you wrote complete sentences.

Quick Write

Think of something you would like for your school or community. Write two sentences telling why it is a good idea. Use at least two spelling words.

A Use the Dictionary: Example Sentence

A dictionary entry lists the meanings of a word. Sometimes, it also gives an example sentence to show how the word is used. Read the entry for the word *reason*.

> **rea•son** /rē zən/
>
> 1. *noun* The cause of something, or the motive behind it. *There was no reason to hurry.* 2. *verb* To think in a logical way. *Aaron reasoned that it would be quicker to walk.*

Write the number of the definition that goes with each example sentence.

_____ We always reason that exercise is good for us.

_____ Mei Ling gave no reason for being late.

B Test Yourself

Write the spelling word that fits the clue.

1. large cat
2. school instruction
3. cause
4. someone
5. used to tie a bow
6. sour fruit
7. cart
8. red-breasted bird
9. relative
10. cottage
11. a small sweet bread
12. gray city bird
13. piano's relative
14. without parents
15. unexpected
16. sea
17. water spray
18. huge hill
19. skipper
20. sure

For Tomorrow...

Get ready to share the words ending in /ən/ that you discovered, and remember to study for the test.

Word Study Strategy

See the word

START

Say it slowly

Link sounds and letters

Write

Check

END

A Link to the Past

Complete each sentence with a spelling word from the box.

picture   fossil   creature   person   reason

What kind of living (1) might have existed a million years ago? To find out, a (2) like you can visit a natural history museum. There you will probably find a (3) room where the remains of ancient animals, such as dinosaurs, are kept. By studying these fossils, you can put together a (4) of the past. Learning more about life long ago is one (5) why many people are interested in fossil remains.

happen   even   structure   temperature   certain

Fossils can tell us many things. We learn about the size and (6) of living things and when they existed. Many fossils show only part of a living thing, but scientists have found (7) animals and plants that are completely preserved. How did this (8) ? One reason is the cold (9) of the Arctic. It (10) helped preserve several woolly mammoths. The natural deep freeze kept woolly mammoths' remains perfectly frozen for thousands of years.

bottom   over   adventure   ocean   mountain

Searching for fossils can be a real (11) . You can find them at the top of a (12) or at the (13) of an (14) . As you learn more about fossils, you will find that these remains of ancient plants and animals are found all (15) the world—from the frozen north to the hot, dry lands of the desert.

captain chapter
lion pigeon
caterpillar hotel
dinner spider
cousin tuna

Relationships

Write the spelling word that completes each group.

1. cocoon, butterfly, _____

2. robin, sparrow, _____

3. uncle, aunt, _____

4. shark, swordfish, _____

5. leader, commander, _____

6. beetle, ant, _____

7. inn, motel, _____

8. title, table of contents, _____

9. tiger, leopard, _____

10. breakfast, lunch, _____

Word Clues

seller blizzard elevator final furniture
literature dollar tiny mirror wagon

Write the spelling word that fits each clue.

11. It's twenty nickels or ten dimes. _____

12. It's a kind of storm. _____

13. It sounds like c*ellar.* _____

14. It takes you to the top. _____

15. It's something you read. _____

16. It's always last. _____

17. It reflects you. _____

18. It's smaller than small. _____

19. It's a four-wheeler that can be pulled
by a horse. _____

20. It's a lamp and a couch. _____

Brain Teaser

Rearrange all the letters in *reward* to spell a new word that answers the riddle.

What do you find in a desk and at an art class?

a _____

adventure   pleasure
basket   reason
better   silver
certain   summer
flavor   super
notice   treasure
pattern   winter
picture   dollar

Tip
Make sure that the sentence subject agrees with the verb.

PROOFREADING MARKS
∧ Add
⊙ Add a period
ℓ Take out
⌒ Move
≡ Capital letter
/ Small letter
¶ Indent paragraph

It Sounds Great!

Catalog descriptions make a product sound special. Write the first two sentences of a catalog description for each item. Use at least two spelling words in your sentences.

1. Snappy Sneakers

_____

_____

2. Meow-Wow Cat Food

_____

_____

3. Whizzer Ice Skates

_____

_____

4. Buckle-On Backpack

_____

_____

5. Snappy Camera

_____

_____

Look back at My Words and the words you misspelled in your Unit 3 Posttests. Use them in another description.

6. Be-a-Brain Computer Game

_____

_____

Those Special Details

Write a detailed catalog description. Proofread for spelling, capitalization, and punctuation.

The Dollar Adventure

The /ər/ sound can be spelled in more than one way. Write the word with /ər/ that completes each sentence.

> **calendar cellar dollar silver**

1. Last Friday I went downstairs to the _____.

2. In a jar I found some very old _____ coins.

3. One of the most unusual coins was a _____.

4. I marked that fantastic day on my _____.

> **letter picture supper treasure**

5. Then I wrote a _____ to a coin collector.

6. I took a _____ of the coin with my camera.

7. I told her about discovering this _____.

8. The collector called one night before I ate _____.

> **better capture over paper super**

9. She told me to advertise the coin in the _____.

10. That way I might _____ a buyer's attention.

11. It wasn't long until I received a _____ offer.

12. Then I sold the coin, and my adventure was _____.

13. I couldn't have asked for a _____ outcome.

Mario says...

Last month I sent a note to my cousin Tina. We were supposed to get together on the weekend. I wrote, "I'll see you on Saturday. We'll have a supper time!"

Tina wrote back and asked what time she was supposed to come to dinner. Was I embarrassed! I had meant to write *super*. It's easy to mix up some words. The good news is that we had a super supper and a super time.

Spelling Matters!

Spelling Words

onion	nation
opinion	relation
million	station
billion	position
stallion	condition
caution	vacation
fashion	discussion
fiction	division
mention	confusion
mansion	conclusion

LOOKOUT WORD

Review	Challenge
pigeon	decision
people	exploration
kitchen	

My Words

_____

_____

_____

_____

Words With ion

A See and Say

The Spelling Concept

/shən/	vacation	nation
/zhən/	division	confusion
/yən/	onion	opinion

The schwa is the sound you hear in an unaccented syllable. In words such as *muffin* and *lemon*, the letters *in* and *on* spell /ən/. In many other words, /ən/ is spelled *ion* as in *onion* and *vacation*.

on + i + on = onion

MEMORY JOGGER

B Link Sounds and Letters

Say each spelling word. Listen for the syllable with /ən/. How is it spelled in each word? Sort the spelling words on a chart like this one.

Word Sort

/shən/	/zhən/	/yən/

C Write and Check

Write the spelling words in the birthday card greeting that end in /ən/.

_____

_____

_____

_____

_____

Birthday Greetings

There is no confusion,
I've reached this conclusion.
It is my opinion
You're one in a million!
No, make that a billion!

Happy Birthday!

Ⓐ Build Vocabulary: Word Meaning

Write the spelling word that matches each meaning.

1. an aunt or uncle
2. a pleasure trip
3. a male horse
4. to tell
5. a thousand thousands
6. a strong-smelling vegetable
7. to warn to be careful
8. a country
9. a thousand millions
10. style of clothing
11. a made-up story
12. a large, fancy house
13. a train stop
14. the place where something is
15. a belief

Ⓑ Word Study: Suffixes

A suffix is a word part added to the end of a word. Add the suffix *-ion* to each base word in ( ) to make a spelling word. You may need to change the spelling of the base word.

16. (discuss) Members of the computer club held a _____.

17. (confuse) There was _____ about how to raise money to buy new computers.

18. (conclude) The members came to this _____ .

19. (divide) There would be a _____ of labor. Some members would plan a fund raiser. Others would advertise it.

Ⓒ Write

Write a question for a poll. Use the words *opinion* and *condition* in your question.

_____

_____

Be a Spelling Sleuth

Look in newspaper ads for words ending in ion such as *vacation* and *television*. Keep a list of the words you find.

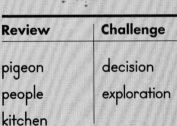

Spell Chat

Challenge your neighbor to think of a word with the suffix -ion and then name a word that rhymes with it. For example, action and reaction.

Spelling Words

onion	nation
opinion	relation
million	station
billion	position
stallion	condition
caution	vacation
fashion	discussion
fiction	division
mention	confusion
mansion *LOOKOUT WORD*	conclusion

Review	Challenge
pigeon	decision
people	exploration
kitchen	

My Words

_____

_____

_____

_____

Spelling Words

onion	nation
opinion	relation
million	station
billion	position
stallion	condition
caution	vacation
fashion	discussion
fiction	division
mention	confusion
LOOKOUT WORD mansion	conclusion

Review	Challenge
pigeon	decision
people	exploration
kitchen	

My Words

Quick Write

In two sentences, tell about a humorous book that you have read recently. Use at least two spelling words.

You may wish to do this activity on a computer.

A Write a Humorous Story

Imagine you woke up and found a check for a million dollars under your pillow! What would you do? Write the opening paragraph of a story. Use four spelling words.

B Proofread

Ari wrote the opening paragraph of his humorous story. He made four spelling errors, one capitalization error, and one punctuation error. Correct them.

Tip

Use an exclamation mark at the end of a sentence to signal a strong feeling, such as surprise, anger, and delight.

I always wake up with one hand tucked under my pillow. Yesterday I felt a piece of paper in my hand. I was holding a check for one millyon dollars! I screamed? I raced to the kichen to tell my family. What would we do with it? Everyone had an opinon. Should we build a manshin? Should we take a vacation? the discussion ended when I woke up.

PROOFREADING MARKS

∧ Add
⊙ Add a period
ℓ Take out
⟳ Move
≡ Capital letter
/ Small letter
¢ Indent paragraph

Now proofread your paragraph. Check your spelling, punctuation, and capitalization.

Ⓐ Use the Dictionary: **Word History**

Dictionaries give the history of some words. The word history may tell you when a word was first used and how its meaning has changed over time. Read the history of the word *onion*.

> **Word History**
>
> The word **onion** comes from the Latin word *unio*, which means "oneness" or "union." If you cut an onion in half, you'll find out why. This vegetable is a "union" of many different layers.

What language does the word *onion* come from? _____

What does the word *unio* mean? _____

Why was an onion named for the word *unio*?

_____

_____

Ⓑ Test Yourself

Fill in the missing letters and write the spelling word.

1. on ___
2. fic ___
3. discus ___
4. mil ___
5. cau ___
6. men ___
7. confu ___
8. na ___
9. opin ___
10. stal ___
11. rela ___
12. fash ___
13. bil ___
14. conclu ___
15. condi ___
16. sta ___
17. posi ___
18. man ___
19. divi ___
20. vaca ___

For Tomorrow... Get ready to share the **ion** words you discovered in ads, and remember to study for your test.

Get Word Wise

A *million* is one thousand thousands. It comes from the Latin word *mille*, meaning "thousand." Another word in the *mille* word family is *millipede*. This wormlike animal looks like it has a thousand feet. *Millennium* is also in the family. A *millennium* is a thousand years.

Word Study Strategy

See the word

START

Say it slowly

Link sounds and letters

Write

Check

END

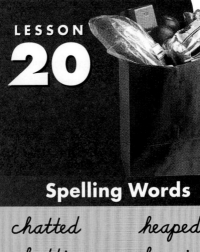

Spelling Words

chatted	heaped
chatting	heaping
cheated	nodded
cheating	nodding
dropped	needed
dropping	needing
drooped	shopped
drooping *LOOKOUT WORD*	shopping
hugged	shouted
hugging	shouting

Review	Challenge
mansion	applauded
chatter	developing
tripped	

My Words

_____

_____

_____

_____

_____

_____

Learn and Spell

Adding -ed and -ing

A See and Say

The Spelling Concept

| chat | chatted | chatting |
| need | needed | needing |

If a one-syllable verb has a short vowel sound and ends in a consonant, double the consonant before adding -ed or -ing.

DD nodded.

MEMORY JOGGER

B Link Sounds and Letters

Say each spelling word. Listen for the vowel sound. Is it long or short? Make a chart like this one. Write the base word of each spelling word in the correct column. Then write the related spelling words with -ed and -ing endings beside it.

Word Sort

Double Consonant			Single Consonant		
bat	batted	batting	heat	heated	heating

C Write and Check

Write the spelling word in the riddle. Then use two spelling words to write a sentence about an elephant in a mall.

_____

_____

_____

_____

RIDDLE

Where are you most likely to find an elephant at the shopping mall?

In the trunk department

Ⓐ Build Vocabulary: Using Verbs

Write the *-ed* or *-ing* form of the verb in ( ) to complete each sentence correctly.

1. Last week I (need) new sneakers for school.

2. I (drop) down onto the couch beside Dad.

3. "Are we (shop) for shoes tonight?" I asked.

4. Then I (heap) some money I'd saved on the couch.

5. Dad was smiling and (nod) cheerfully.

6. That evening we (shop) in several shoe stores.

7. After I chose my new shoes, I (hug) Dad.

8. He asked if I was happy, and I (nod).

Spell Chat

Say a one-syllable verb with -ing and -ed added. Ask the person next to you to use the words in a sentence.

Ⓑ Word Study: Analogies

Look at the relationship between the words. Write the spelling word that completes the sentence.

9. *Pouted* is to *pouting*, as *shouted* is to ____.

10. *Bat* is to *batting*, as *chat* is to ____.

11. *Feed* is to *feeding*, as *need* is to ____.

12. *Pat* is to *patted*, as *chat* is to ____.

13. *Leap* is to *leaping*, as *heap* is to____.

14. *Spout* is to *spouted*, as *shout* is to ____.

15. *Seat* is to *seated*, as *cheat* is to____.

16. *Loop* is to *looping*, as *droop* is to ____.

17. *Greet* is to *greeting*, as *cheat* is to ____.

18. *Shop* is to *shopping*, as *drop* is to ____.

19. *Stoop* is to *stooped*, as *droop* is to ____.

20. *Chug* is to *chugging*, as *hug* is to ____.

Spelling Words

chatted	heaped
chatting	heaping
cheated	nodded
cheating	nodding
dropped	needed
dropping	needing
drooped	shopped
drooping LOOKOUT WORD	shopping
hugged	shouted
hugging	shouting

Review	Challenge
mansion	applauded
chatter	developing
tripped	

My Words

_____

_____

_____

_____

Quick Write

Write a sentence that contains an exaggeration. Use at least two spelling words.

You may wish to do this activity on a computer.

Ⓐ Write a Cartoon Strip

To exaggerate means to make something sound bigger and more important than it is. Invent two comic strip characters, and write a dialogue in which they exaggerate. Use four spelling words.

Ⓑ Proofread

Tanya wrote the dialogue for her comic strip. She made three spelling errors, two punctuation errors, and one capitalization error. Correct her errors.

Tip
Use commas to separate three or more words in a series. For example, I bought bananas, apples, and oranges.

Matt: Why are you shoutting, Pat?
Pat: I triped over a cat the size of an elephant and dropped these books.
Matt: can I help you?
Pat: Sure! Help me deliver the books to Kim Mike, and Katie.
Matt: No problem! Start heeping them into my backpack
Pat: Thanks a heap!

PROOFREADING MARKS

∧ Add
⊙ Add a period
ℓ Take out
◯⁀ Move
≡ Capital letter
/ Small letter
¶ Indent paragraph

Now proofread your dialogue. Check for spelling, capitalization, and punctuation.

Get Word Wise

Have you ever heard of a "dropped egg"? The term was first used in 1824. A cook would bring water to a boil and then crack an egg and drop in the white and yolk. Today we call this a "poached egg."

Ⓐ Use the Thesaurus: Synonyms and Antonyms

A thesaurus is a book with a collection of synonyms. Some thesauruses also give antonyms. A thesaurus can help you find colorful words to use in your writing. Here are thesaurus entries for *droop* and *shout*.

> **droop** *verb* wilt, hang

> **shout** *verb* scream, yell
> *antonym* whisper

Write a sentence, using one of the synonyms of *droop*.

_____

_____

Write a sentence with a synonym for *shout*. Write another sentence in which you use an antonym for *shout*.

_____

_____

Ⓑ Test Yourself

Add the ending to each base word to make a spelling word. Remember to double the last consonant if it follows a short vowel. Write the word.

1. shop + ing	**8.** nod + ing	**15.** nod + ed
2. droop + ed	**9.** shout + ing	**16.** heap + ing
3. cheat + ing	**10.** chat + ed	**17.** shop + ed
4. need + ed	**11.** need + ing	**18.** droop + ing
5. drop + ing	**12.** shout + ed	**19.** hug + ing
6. heap + ed	**13.** chat + ing	**20.** cheat + ed
7. hug + ed	**14.** drop + ed	

For Tomorrow...
Get ready to share the verbs with **-ed** and **-ing** you discovered, and remember to study for your test!

Word Study Strategy

START
See the word
Say it slowly
Link sounds and letters
Write
Check
END

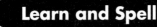
Learn and Spell

Final e With -ed and -ing

A See and Say

Spelling Words

damaged pleased
damaging pleasing
decided promised
deciding promising
divided stared
dividing staring
giggled traded
giggling trading
noticed teased
noticing teasing

LOOKOUT WORD

Review	Challenge
drooping	shuffled
happen	rhyming
wasted	

My Words

_____

_____

_____

The Spelling Concept

notice + ing = noticing
notice + ed = noticed

Some verbs end with an e. Drop the e before adding *-ed* or *-ing*.

Is **Ed** where he promised to be?

MEMORY JOGGER

B Link Sounds and Letters

Say each spelling word. Listen for the ending sound. Then say its base word, and write it in the first column on a chart like this one. Write the word with *-ed* in the second column and with *-ing* in the third column.

Word Sort		
Base Word	-ed	-ing

C Write and Check

Write the spelling words that are in the answer to the riddle.

_____

_____

RIDDLE

What did one math problem say to another?

You promised we wouldn't be divided.

Vocabulary Practice

A Build Vocabulary: Using Verbs

Add *-ing* or *-ed* to each word in ( ) to complete the
sentences correctly.

1. Tina was (stare) at the community garden.
2. It was (damage) during the heavy storm.
3. People (notice) how much damage had been done.
4. Everyone was (promise) to help with the cleanup.
5. Adam (stare) sadly at the fallen tree.
6. We were (please) to see everyone help.
7. People (trade) jobs with each other.
8. Friends and neighbors were (divide) the tasks.
9. We all (decide) we were glad the storm was over.

Spell Chat

Challenge your neighbor to think of another verb that ends with **e**, such as *tumble*, and to spell the **-ed** and **-ing** forms of the word.

B Word Study: Synonyms

Write the spelling word that is a synonym of each
of these words.

10. joked
11. joking
12. vowed
13. harming
14. choosing
15. laughing
16. separated
17. seeing
18. delighting
19. exchanging
20. chuckled

C Write

Write this sentence and finish it: Jeff promised _____.
Then write another sentence using another spelling word
in place of *promised*.

_____

_____

Be a Spelling Sleuth

Look in children's magazines and poetry books for verbs with -ed or -ing in which the final e was dropped. For example, *promised, wiggled* and *skating*.

Spelling Words

damaged	pleased
damaging	pleasing
decided	promised *LOOKOUT WORD*
deciding	promising
divided	stared
dividing	staring
giggled	traded
giggling	trading
noticed	teased
noticing	teasing

Review	Challenge
drooping	shuffled
happen	rhyming
wasted	

My Words

_____

_____

_____

_____

Spelling Words

damaged	pleased
damaging	pleasing
decided	promised
deciding	promising
divided	stared
dividing	staring
giggled	traded
giggling	trading
noticed	teased
noticing	teasing

Review	Challenge
drooping	shuffled
happen	rhyming
wasted	

My Words

_____

_____

_____

_____

Quick Write

Write two sentences about a TV show or movie you like. Use two spelling words.

You may wish to do this activity on a computer.

Ⓐ Write Interview Questions

Imagine you are a TV talk-show host. Choose an interesting person to interview. Write three questions that will give your audience a new view of this person. Use four spelling words in your questions.

Ⓑ Proofread

Eric wrote three interview questions to ask his favorite actor. He made four spelling errors and a punctuation error. He also forgot to capitalize a word in a title. Correct the errors.

Tip
Capitalize all important words in books or movie titles.

1. I read that you decideed to be an actor when you were ten. How did that happen?

2. You starred in Happy times, The Promised Land, and Tradeing Post. Which movie is your favorite?

3. I notised that you've won a lot of awards. You must feel very pleased. Which award are you most proud of

PROOFREADING MARKS

∧ Add
⊙ Add a period
ℓ Take out
○⌒ Move
≡ Capital letter
∕ Small letter
¶ Indent paragraph

Now proofread your interview questions. Check spelling and punctuation, and capitalization in any titles.

Ⓐ Use the Dictionary: Guide Words

The two words at the top of each page in a dictionary are guide words. Guide words tell you the first entry word and last entry word that appear on the page.

> **squeeze ▶ staff**
>
> **squeeze** /skwēz/ *verb*
> To press something firmly together from opposite sides.

Look at each pair of dictionary guide words. Write the spelling words that would be on each page.

dark•diner _____

play•protect _____

Write two spelling words. Then look up each word in the Spelling Dictionary. Write the guide words for each word.

_____

_____

Ⓑ Test Yourself

Figure out the missing vowels and write each spelling word.

1. tr_d_d
2. tr_d_ng
3. pl__s_d
4. pl__s_ng
5. d_m_g_d
6. d_m_g_ng
7. st_r_d
8. st_r_ng
9. g_ggl_d
10. g_ggl_ng
11. pr_m_s_d
12. pr_m_s_ng
13. n_t_c_d
14. n_t_c_ng
15. d_v_d_d
16. d_v_d_ng
17. d_c_d_d
18. d_c_d_ng
19. t__s_d
20. t__s_ng

For Tomorrow...
Get ready to share the **-ed** and **-ing** forms of verbs you discovered. Remember to study for your test!

Get Word Wise
The verb *promise* means to give one's word to do something. *Promising* is a form of the verb *promise*. The word *promising* can also be an adjective with another meaning. You might say *She has a promising career* or *He is a promising student*. In these sentences, *promising* means "to do well or be successful."

Word Study Strategy

START

See the word

Say it slowly

Link sounds and letters

Write

Check

END

LESSON 22

Spelling Words

cried
crying
copied
copying
denied LOOKOUT WORD
denying
emptied
emptying
fried
frying

married
marrying
buried
burying
spied
spying
replied
replying
supplied
supplying

Review	Challenge
promised	satisfied
notice	multiplying
hurried	

My Words

Changing Final y to i

A See and Say

The Spelling Concept

copy + ed = copied
copy + ing = copying

When a verb ends with a consonant + y, change the y to i before adding -ed. Do not change the y when you add -ing.

Do you spy the **pie** in s**pie**d?

MEMORY JOGGER

B Link Sounds and Letters

Say each spelling word. Listen for the word ending. Write the base word of each spelling word in the first column of a chart like this one. Then write the word with -ed and -ing endings.

Word Sort

Base Word hurry	-ed hurried	-ing hurrying

C Write and Check

Write the spelling word that appears in this brain teaser.

BRAIN TEASER

Where does emptying come before filling?

In the dictionary

Ⓐ Build Vocabulary: **Antonyms**

Antonyms, such as *high* and *low*, are words that have opposite meanings. A computer made a mistake and put the wrong word or phrase in each sentence. Write the spelling word that is an antonym for each underlined word or phrase.

1. I <u>admitted</u> I was wrong.

2. I was <u>laughing</u> at the sad news.

3. He <u>filled</u> the overflowing basket.

4. They were <u>admitting</u> that they liked the movie.

5. The dog <u>dug up</u> a bone.

6. They <u>laughed</u> when their team lost.

7. She was <u>filling</u> the garbage can.

8. I was <u>digging up</u> the treasure chest.

> **Spell Chat**
> Challenge a classmate to think of another verb that ends with a consonant followed by **y**, and to write the word with the endings **-ed** and **-ing**.

Ⓑ Word Study: **Verb Forms**

Solve these word problems by writing the spelling words.

9. copy + ed = _____

10. spy + ing = _____

11. reply + ing = _____

12. supply + ed = _____

13. copy + ing = _____

14. marry + ed = _____

15. supply + ing = _____

16. reply + ed = _____

17. fry + ing = _____

18. marry + ing = _____

19. spy + ed = _____

20. fry + ed = _____

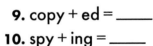

Ⓒ Write

Use these words to write the first two sentences of a newspaper article.

hurried   spied   promised

_____

_____

_____

_____

Spelling Words

cried	married
crying	marrying
copied	buried
copying	burying
denied *LOOKOUT WORD*	spied
denying	spying
emptied	replied
emptying	replying
fried	supplied
frying	supplying

Review	Challenge
promised	satisfied
notice	multiplying
hurried	

My Words

_____

_____

_____

_____

You may wish to do this activity on a computer.

Spelling Words

cried	married
crying	marrying
copied	buried
copying	burying
denied (LOOKOUT WORD)	spied
denying	spying
emptied	replied
emptying	replying
fried	supplied
frying	supplying

Review	Challenge
promised	satisfied
notice	multiplying
hurried	

My Words

Quick Write

Write an exaggeration about a food you saw or ate. For example, you might exaggerate its size, color, or taste. Use at least two spelling words.

Ⓐ Write a Tall Tale

Tall tales are fun to read because they use exaggeration to make them humorous. Write the beginning of a tall tale. Think of a character to star in it. What amazing and unusual things can this character do? Use at least three spelling words in your tale.

Ⓑ Proofread

Alexa wrote the beginning of a tall tale. She made three spelling errors and one punctuation error. She also forgot an apostrophe in a word. Correct the errors.

Tip
When you write a contraction, use an apostrophe in place of the letters that have been dropped.

> "I'm hungry as a bear!" hollered Abilene Annie. She cooked up a stack of pancakes as high as a skyscraper. "Oh, no!" she cryed. "I cant have pancakes without syrup." She yanked out the bathtub and hurryed to the woods. She began empting every maple tree in the forest of syrup until her bathtub overflowed

Now proofread your sentences. Check your spelling, punctuation, and use of contractions.

PROOFREADING MARKS

∧ Add
⊙ Add a period
ℓ Take out
ↄↄ Move
≡ Capital letter
/ Small letter
¶ Indent paragraph

Ⓐ Use the Dictionary: **Word Endings**

Suppose you want to look up the spelling of *fried* in the dictionary? Adjectives and verbs that end in *-ed* or *-ing* are usually listed under the base word. To find out how to spell *fried*, you'd have to look up *fry*. Read the entry.

> **fry** /frī/ *verb*
> To cook food in hot fat or oil. ▸ **fries, frying, fried**
> ▸ *adjective* **fried**

Write the words that are verb forms of *fry*.

_____ _____ _____

Which word is an adjective form of *fry*? _____

Write the entry word you would look up in the dictionary to find each of the following words.

replied _____ promised _____

Ⓑ Test Yourself

Choose the ending *-ed* or *-ing* that completes each word. Then write the spelling word.

1. reply___	**8.** repli___	**15.** cri___
2. fri___	**9.** marry___	**16.** spy___
3. cry___	**10.** deni___	**17.** suppli___
4. spi___	**11.** copy___	**18.** copi___
5. empti___	**12.** bury___	**19.** buri___
6. deny___	**13.** marri___	**20.** supply___
7. fry___	**14.** empty___	

For Tomorrow...
Get ready to share the -ed and -ing verb forms you discovered, and remember to study for your test!

Get Word Wise

Today the word *copy* means "to reproduce an original." It comes from the Latin word *copia*, which means "abundance" or "plenty." When we make *copies* of an original, we then have more than one, or plenty.

Word Study Strategy

See the word

START

Say it slowly

Link sounds and letters

Write

Check

END

LESSON 23

Spelling Words

forget	wrote
forgot	written
forgotten	drove
forgive	driven
forgave	knew
forgiven	known
broke	threw
broken	thrown
spoke	drew
spoken	drawn — LOOKOUT WORD

Review	Challenge
denied	forbidden
creature	withdrawn
heard	

My Words

Irregular Verbs

A See and Say

The Spelling Concept

I forget.   I forgot.   I have forgotten.

Irregular verbs have special forms to show the past tense. They do not add *-ed*.

> Remember the three words in **forgotten**— **for got ten.**
>
> MEMORY JOGGER

B Link Sounds and Letters

Say each spelling word in a sentence. Decide which verb is in the present tense, which is in the past tense, and which shows the past tense with a helping verb. Sort the words on a chart like this one.

Word Sort

Present Today I...	Past Yesterday I...	Past With Helping Verb I have...

C Write and Check

Solve each word math puzzle. Write the spelling word. Then use three other words and make up your own puzzles.

_____

_____

_____

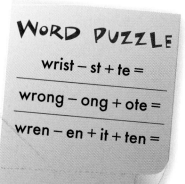

WORD PUZZLE

wrist – st + te = _____

wrong – ong + ote = _____

wren – en + it + ten = _____

Vocabulary Practice

Ⓐ Build Vocabulary: Irregular Verbs

Write the correct verb form to complete each sentence.

1. Last night I _____ to put my library book in my backpack.

2. I had _____ myself a note to remind me.

3. I had also _____ a picture of a book on it.

4. I had even _____ to my dad, asking him to remind me.

5. As he _____ away this morning, he shouted something at me.

6. "What?" I asked. He didn't reply because he had already _____ away.

7. Since I didn't have my book, I _____ the librarian a note.

8. She has kindly _____ other students for returning books late.

9. She _____ me, too.

Spell Chat

Challenge the person next to you to name as many **irregular verbs** as possible in 60 seconds. Hints: *fly, choose, write, fall.*

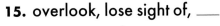

Ⓑ Word Study: Relationships

Write the verb that best completes each group. None of the answers take helping verbs.

10. understood, realized, ___
11. painted, colored, ___
12. flung, tossed, ___
13. talked, chatted, ___
14. cracked, shattered, ___
15. overlook, lose sight of, ___
16. excuse, pardon, ___

Ⓒ Write

Write an ad for a secondhand store. Use the words *known, thrown, forgotten,* and *broken.*

_____

_____

_____

Spelling Words

forget	wrote
forgot	written
forgotten	drove
forgive	driven
forgave	knew
forgiven	known
broke	threw
broken	thrown
spoke	drew
spoken	drawn

LOOKOUT WORD

Review	Challenge
denied	forbidden
creature	withdrawn
heard	

My Words

_____
_____
_____
_____

Quick Write

Write something nice that a friend has said or might say to you. Use at least two spelling words.

You may wish to do this activity on a computer.

A Write a Description

Write a paragraph about a person you admire. It could be a friend, favorite performer, writer, or artist. Describe what this person does. Use at least three spelling words. Include a quotation in your paragraph that tells something you or your subject might say.

B Proofread

Carmen wrote a paragraph about one of her friends. She made four spelling errors, one verb-tense error, and one punctuation error. Correct the errors.

Tip
Use a comma to separate a quotation from the rest of the sentence.

> My friend Rashid is an amazing artist. Once I threw out an old hose and some boxes that had brokn. Before I know it, Rashid used them to build a funny-looking creture that won an art contest. Last week I spok to Rashid about his imaginative ideas. He said "I haven't forgoten the great stuff you gave me. Your junk became my treasure!"

Now proofread your sentences. Check spelling and punctuation.

PROOFREADING MARKS

∧ Add
⊙ Add a period
ℓ Take out
⟳ Move
≡ Capital letter
/ Small letter
¶ Indent paragraph

Study and Review

ⓐ Use the Dictionary: **Idioms**

An idiom is a commonly used phrase that means something different from what it appears to mean. For example, if a homework assignment is "a piece of cake," it means that it is easy. Read the dictionary entry for *throw*.

> **throw** /thrō/
> 1. *verb* To send through the air; fling, hurl.
> 2. *idiom* If something **throws** you, it confuses you.

Write a sentence, using the idiom "threw me."

_____

Look up the word *speak* in your Spelling Dictionary.
Write a sentence for the idiom "speak up" or "speak out."

_____

_____

ⓑ Test Yourself

Write the spelling word hidden in each group of letters.

1. almbrokez
2. rsforgotten
3. ouswrote
4. tlydroveble
5. dioknewmnr
6. yzwrittenfr
7. oefspoken
8. rvudrivenxe
9. abcthrewxy
10. fdeforgiveptu
11. mladrawnjk
12. opqforgiven
13. thrownihalt
14. todcebroken
15. rstuvaspoke
16. forgetoemr
17. amftuforgot
18. zyknownst
19. oqudrewjel
20. wforgaveyou

> **For Tomorrow...**
> Get ready to share the **irregular verbs** you discovered, and remember to study for your test!

Get Word Wise

At some time, you have probably drawn a picture or drawn the curtains in your home. How can the word *draw* be used to describe different actions? The word's history answers the question. *Draw* comes from an Old Norse word meaning "to drag." When you draw with a pencil, you drag it across paper. When you draw the curtains, you drag them across a rod.

Word Study Strategy

START
See the word
Say it slowly
Link sounds and letters
Write
Check
END

A PARTY to Remember

Write the spelling word to complete each sentence.

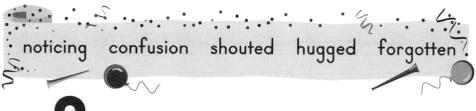

written   shopping   decided   divided   promised

The Perez children—Maria, Juan, and Lucia—all __(1)__ to have a surprise party for their mother. There was a lot to do, so they __(2)__ up the chores and asked their father and aunts and uncles to help. Aunt Isabel said she would make sure the invitations were __(3)__ and mailed out. Papa __(4)__ to rent a tent and set it up in the backyard. Uncle Felipe agreed to take the children __(5)__ for food and decorations.

noticing   confusion   shouted   hugged   forgotten

On the day of the party, things were in a state of __(6)__ . Everyone hurried from place to place, making sure no details were __(7)__ . They were so busy, Mama walked right in without anyone even __(8)__ ! "What's going on?" she asked. Everyone __(9)__ , "Surprise!" Then they __(10)__ her and congratulated her on her new job.

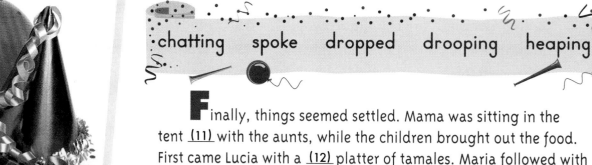

chatting   spoke   dropped   drooping   heaping

Finally, things seemed settled. Mama was sitting in the tent __(11)__ with the aunts, while the children brought out the food. First came Lucia with a __(12)__ platter of tamales. Maria followed with the cake, while Juan carried the fruit punch. That's when it happened. Juan tripped and spilled the punch. The noise startled Maria, and she __(13)__ the cake. Then Lucia bumped into a tent pole, and the whole tent started __(14)__ . Nobody __(15)__ a word. Finally, Mama smiled. "Well! This is a party that's just full of surprises!"

Synonyms

Synonyms are words that have the same or nearly the same meaning. Write the synonym for the underlined word in each sentence.

1. In May I <u>spotted</u> a poster for a reading fair. _____

2. Last week I was there <u>swapping</u> comic books. _____

3. This is the best fair in the <u>country</u>. _____

4. I was <u>happy</u> that I was able to go. _____

5. It was fun <u>talking</u> with other comic collectors. _____

6. By the fair's <u>end</u>, I had two new friends and a pile of new books. _____

7. I will not <u>overlook</u> the great time we had. _____

8. Today I <u>penned</u> a letter to each friend. _____

Analogies

Write the word that completes each analogy.

9. *Catch* is to *caught*, as *throw* is to _____.

10. *Sneaker* is to *shoe*, as _____ is to *building*.

11. *Addition* is to *subtraction*, as *multiplication* is to _____.

12. *Folk song* is to *music*, as _____ is to *writing*.

13. *Smiled* is to *frowned*, as *filled* is to _____.

14. *Copy* is to *copied*, as *marry* is to _____.

15. *Knowing* is to *known*, as *drawing* is to _____.

16. *See* is to *seen*, as *speak* is to _____.

17. *Ending* is to *finishing*, as *yelling* is to _____.

Letter Puzzle

Write the letter that's in both words. Then write the word that answers the riddle.

fit and fan ____

rope and rib ____

sit and tie ____

pen and wet ____

hid and do ____

When does an Idaho potato change its nationality?

when it's French

____ ____ ____ ____ ____

onion	shouted
nation	million
vacation	heaping
mansion	drooping
condition	deciding
pleased	broken
forgotten	frying
threw	drove

Tip
When you write verbs with the endings **-ed** and **-ing,** check to see if you need to make a spelling change.

PROOFREADING MARKS

∧ Add
⊙ Add a period
ℓ Take out
∽ Move
≡ Capital letter
/ Small letter
¶ Indent paragraph

Picture This

A photographer wrote some notes for her photos that will appear in a local newspaper. You are the reporter who has to turn the notes into sentences for captions. Use at least two spelling words in each sentence.

1. Grownups and children at the beach

_____

_____

2. The pitcher and batter in a softball game

_____

_____

3. An old house

_____

_____

4. A cook at a fourth of July barbecue in the park

_____

_____

5. Crowds greeting the woman who walked cross-country

_____

_____

Look back at My Words and the words you misspelled in your Unit 4 Posttests. Use them to write another caption.

6. Hundreds of people turn out for parade

_____

The Big Story

Write the first paragraph of a news story to go along with one of the captions you wrote. Use three spelling words. Proofread for spelling, capitalization, and punctuation. Then share the article with a classmate.

Cleaning Up

Look at the base word in ( ) in each sentence. Add *-ed* or *-ing* to complete the sentence. Write the word.

cried	noticed	chatting	promised	replied
decided	dropping	supplied	denying	shopped
needed	heaped	pleased	copying	

1. _____ Last spring my class (**notice**) the trash in Roaring Creek.

2. _____ We (**decide**) to clean up the creek on Earth Day.

3. _____ We (**shop**) for the supplies we needed.

4. _____ We told everyone we knew that we (**need**) help.

5. _____ Many people (**reply**) that they would join us.

6. _____ On Earth Day people kept (**drop**) by all the time.

7. _____ We (**heap**) the trash into bags.

8. _____ Restaurants (**supply**) us with sandwiches.

9. _____ We were so busy there was not even a minute for (**chat**).

10. _____ Cleaning up Roaring Creek by sunset (**please**) everyone.

11. _____ "We're finished!" we (**cry**) happily.

12. _____ There's no (**deny**) that we did a good job.

13. _____ Now other schools in our area are (**copy**) our example.

14. _____ We (**promise**) each other to do it again next year.

Learn and Spell

More Irregular Verbs

A See and Say

Spelling Words

creep
crept
sleep
slept
mean
meant
wind
wound
leave
left

catch
caught
teach
taught
buy
bought
bring
brought
build
built

LOOKOUT
WORD

Review	Challenge
drawn	seek
cousin	sought
frighten	

My Words

The Spelling Concept

Present Tense	Past Tense
creep	crept
leave	left

Many verbs add -ed to show past tense. Past-tense verbs that do not add -ed are irregular.

Will **u** buy it?

MEMORY JOGGER

B Link Sounds and Letters

Say each pair of spelling words. Then write the words. Use the sentence starters to help you sort the present-tense verbs and the past-tense verbs on a chart like this one.

Word Sort

Today I...	Yesterday I...

C Write and Check

Write the spelling words that are in the riddle.

_____

_____

RIDDLE

Why did the cowgirl wind her watch at the end of the cattle drive?

(round up)
Because it was the
last wound up

A Build Vocabulary: **Antonyms**

Write a spelling word that is the antonym, or opposite, of the underlined word. Remember that your answer must be the same verb tense as the clue.

1. <u>arrived</u> early
2. <u>awakened</u> past dawn
3. <u>throw</u> a football
4. <u>sold</u> a bike
5. <u>hurried</u> up the stairs
6. <u>tear down</u> a wall
7. <u>threw</u> a baseball
8. <u>arrive</u> today
9. <u>tore down</u> a house
10. <u>unwound</u> the string
11. <u>learned</u> Spanish
12. <u>sell</u> a toy

> **Spell Chat**
>
> Give a classmate a clue for a spelling word. Ask the classmate to name both the present- and past-tense forms of the verb that fits the clue.

B Word Study: **Adjectives**

You can turn many verbs into adjectives by adding -*y* or -*ing*. Add the ending in ( ) to a word below to complete each phrase. Write the adjective.

teach   wind   sleep   creep

13. tired and ___ (y)
14. steep and ___ (ing)
15. scary and ___ (y)
16. training and ___ (ing)

C Write

Write a question and answer for each pair of spelling words.

bring brought   mean meant

_____

_____

Be a Spelling Sleuth

Look in news magazines and newspapers for verbs that have an **irregular past** tense. For example, *lend* and *lent*, *leave* and *left*, *build* and *built*. Keep a list.

Spelling Words

creep	catch
crept	caught
sleep	teach
slept	taught
mean	buy
meant	bought
wind	bring
wound	brought
leave	build
left	built

Review	Challenge
drawn	seek
cousin	sought
frighten	

My Words

_____

_____

_____

_____

You may wish to do this activity on a computer.

Spelling Words

creep	catch
crept	caught
sleep	teach
slept	taught
mean	buy **LOOKOUT WORD**
meant	bought
wind	bring
wound	brought
leave	build
left	built

Review	Challenge
drawn	seek
cousin	sought
frighten	

My Words

Quick Write

Write about something you built. What was it? What did you do to build it? Use two spelling words.

Ⓐ Write a Journal Entry

Write a journal entry about an outdoor adventure you've had or imagined, such as a trip or an outdoor sleepover. Where did you go? What did you hear and see? Use four spelling words.

Ⓑ Proofread

Tony wrote this journal entry. He made three spelling errors, one punctuation error, and left out part of a verb. Correct the errors.

Tip
Remember that the verb *saw* stands alone while *seen* needs a helper such as *has* or *have*.

Last night my cuzin Julio and I sleeped in his backyard. We brout snacks and talked for hours. I never seen such bright stars! Much later, I woke up and saw a shape. It crept toward us. I yelled, and Julio woke up Something jumped between us and barked. The shape was Bear, Julio's dog. He wanted to sleep out, too.

Now proofread your journal entry. Check your spelling, punctuation, and verbs.

PROOFREADING MARKS

∧ Add
⊙ Add a period
ℓ Take out
↶↷ Move
≡ Capital letter
／ Small letter
¶ Indent paragraph

Study and Review

Ⓐ Use the Dictionary: Irregular Verbs

How do you find the meaning or spelling of an irregular past-tense verb? Look up the present tense of the verb. Read these entries. Notice how the past-tense verbs are shown.

> **teach** /tēch/ *verb*
> To give a lesson, or to show someone how to do something. ▶ **teaches, teaching, taught**

> **catch** /kach/ *verb*
> To grab hold of something moving through the air, as in *to catch a ball.* ▶ **catches, catching, caught**

Write the entry word you would look up to find each of these irregular past-tense verbs. Check your answers in the Spelling Dictionary.

bought _____   wound _____

left _____   built _____

crept _____   slept _____

brought _____   caught _____

Ⓑ Test Yourself

Figure out the vowels that have been left out of each spelling word. Write the complete word.

1. cr _ _ p
2. b _ _ ld
3. l _ _ v _
4. cr _ pt
5. t _ _ ch
6. b _ _ ght
7. m _ _ n
8. c _ tch
9. b _ y
10. br _ ng

11. w _ _ nd
12. sl _ pt
13. t _ _ ght
14. br _ _ ght
15. l _ ft
16. b _ _ lt
17. sl _ _ p
18. m _ _ nt
19. w _ nd
20. c _ _ ght

For Tomorrow...
Get ready to share the **irregular verbs** you discovered, and remember to study for your test!

Word Study Strategy

See the word — START
Say it slowly
Link sounds and letters
Write
Check
END

Spelling Words

altogether *LOOKOUT WORD*   lifetime
broadcast   notebook
cardboard   paperback
daylight   pushover
earthquake   runway
flashback   skateboard
hardware   splashdown
headache   sweatshirt
headquarters   toothbrush
leftover   watermelon

Review	Challenge
buy	nevertheless
mention	merry-go-round
homework	

My Words

Compound Words

Ⓐ See and Say

The Spelling Concept

life + time = lifetime
note + book = notebook
left + over = leftover

Words made from two smaller words are called *compound words*. The smaller words are often written together as one word. Usually the spelling of the smaller words does not change when they are combined.

> When **all** and **together** get together, they leave one l behind.
>
> MEMORY JOGGER

Ⓑ Link Sounds and Letters

Say each spelling word. Listen for the two smaller words that make up the compound word. On a chart like the one shown, write each compound word. Then write the two words that make up the compound word.

Word Sort

Compound Word	Smaller Words

Ⓒ Write and Check

Find the compound words in the riddle. Write the one that is a spelling word.

_____

RIDDLE

Why did the astronaut wear a swimsuit on his spacecraft?

He wanted to be ready for the splashdown.

A Build Vocabulary: Context Clues

Find the two words in each sentence that go together to make a compound spelling word. Write the compound word.

1. You see light during the day.
2. It was the time of his life.
3. He had an ache in his head.
4. The earth began to quake.
5. The brush was used to clean each tooth.
6. You can skate with this board.
7. You can write a note in this book.
8. The rocket went down with a splash.
9. We put all the pieces together.

> **Spell Chat**
> With a partner, separate a spelling word into its parts. Use one of the parts to make a new **compound word**. For example, *postcard* or *chalkboard* can be made from *cardboard*.

B Word Study: Match Compounds

Look at the underlined word in each compound word. Write the spelling word that also has this smaller word.

10. <u>sweat</u>pants
11. <u>water</u>fall
12. <u>flash</u>bulb
13. <u>paper</u>weight
14. down<u>cast</u>
15. <u>head</u>phones
16. <u>card</u>holder
17. <u>hard</u>ball
18. <u>run</u>around
19. <u>push</u>cart
20. take<u>over</u>

C Write

Use these words in a sentence.

notebook   homework

_____

_____

Be a Spelling Sleuth
Look for compound words on all kinds of signs and labels. For example, *paperback books, volleyball courts, ferryboat docks, birthday cards.* List the words you find.

Spelling Words

altogether *(Lookout Word)*	lifetime
broadcast	notebook
cardboard	paperback
daylight	pushover
earthquake	runway
flashback	skateboard
hardware	splashdown
headache	sweatshirt
headquarters	toothbrush
leftover	watermelon

Review	Challenge
buy	nevertheless
mention	merry-go-round
homework	

My Words

_____

_____

_____

_____

Spelling Words

altogether	lifetime
broadcast	notebook
cardboard	paperback
daylight	pushover
earthquake	runway
flashback	skateboard
hardware	splashdown
headache	sweatshirt
headquarters	toothbrush
leftover	watermelon

Review	Challenge
buy	nevertheless
mention	merry-go-round
homework	

My Words

Quick Write

Write a title for a mystery you'd like to read. Use at least two spelling words.

You may wish to do this activity on a computer.

Ⓐ Write Notes for a Mystery Story

Write notes to help you plan a mystery. What is the problem in your mystery? How is it solved? Use four spelling words in your notes.

Ⓑ Proofread

April wrote notes for a mystery story. She made four spelling errors and one punctuation error. Correct the errors.

Tip
A question always ends with a question mark.

Sam Stone, boy detective, is doing his homewerk when he hears a radio broadkast. A dinosaur bone has disappeared from the museum in broad daylite. Who took it   Only Sam can find out. He grabs his notbook and skateboard and zooms off. He knows he can solve the mystery. By the end of the day, he finds the bone. Professor T. Rex's dog took it!

PROOFREADING MARKS

∧ Add
⊙ Add a period
ℓ Take out
↶ Move
≡ Capital letter
/ Small letter
¶ Indent paragraph

Now proofread your notes.
Check for spelling and punctuation errors.

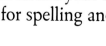

Study and Review

A Use the Dictionary: Parts of Speech

A dictionary entry lists the different meanings of a word. It also tells which parts of speech the word can be. Read the dictionary entry for *broadcast*.

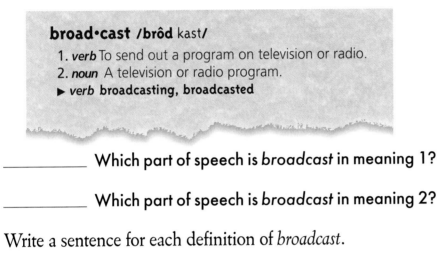

broad•cast /brôd kast/
1. *verb* To send out a program on television or radio.
2. *noun* A television or radio program.
▸ *verb* broadcasting, broadcasted

_____ Which part of speech is *broadcast* in meaning 1?

_____ Which part of speech is *broadcast* in meaning 2?

Write a sentence for each definition of *broadcast*.

_____

_____

B Test Yourself

Figure out the missing part of each compound word. Write the complete spelling word.

1. __ache
2. note__
3. __down
4. earth__
5. __brush
6. al__
7. __melon
8. left__
9. __light
10. paper__
11. __way
12. sweat__
13. __quarters
14. push__
15. __time
16. card__
17. flash__
18. __ware
19. skate__
20. __cast

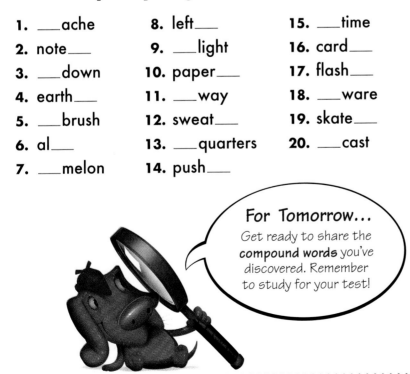

For Tomorrow...
Get ready to share the **compound words** you've discovered. Remember to study for your test!

Get Word Wise

Our modern word *book*, one part of the compound word *notebook*, comes from the Anglo-Saxon word *boc*, which means "beech tree." The Anglo Saxons scratched messages on the smooth bark of these trees.

Word Study Strategy

START

See the word

Say it slowly

Link sounds and letters

Write

Check

END

Words With -er and -est

A See and Say

Spelling Words

busier	colder
busiest	coldest
earlier	stranger
earliest	strangest
funnier	simpler
funniest	simplest
sillier	wetter
silliest	wettest
warmer	sadder
warmest	saddest

LOOKOUT WORD

Review	Challenge
altogether	fiercer
cheated	loveliest
silly	

My Words

_____

_____

_____

The Spelling Concept

cold	colder	coldest
funny	funnier	funniest
sad	sadder	saddest

To compare two things, add -er to the end of a base word. To compare three or more things, add -est. You may need to make a spelling change in the base word before adding -er or -est.

> I am busier than you.

MEMORY JOGGER

B Link Sounds and Letters

Say each spelling word. Listen to the endings. Look for spelling changes when -er and -est are added to the base word. Write the spelling words on a chart like this one.

Word Sort

Changes When Adding -er and -est			
No change	Changed y to i	Dropped Final e	Doubled Final Consonant

C Write and Check

Write the two spelling words that are in the logic puzzle. Then use two other spelling words to make up another puzzle.

_____

_____

LOGIC PUZZLE

Famous Fay is funnier than Friendly Fran, but Famous Fay is not as funny as Fabulous Fred. Who is the funniest?

Fabulous Fred is the funniest.

Vocabulary Practice

A Build Vocabulary: Using Adjectives

Complete the tall tale. Write the correct form of each adjective in ( ) by adding -*er* or -*est*.

The busy people of Lightning Flats are still talking about the (**1.** strange) weather they have ever seen! First came the (**2.** wet) spring in a hundred years. Even the frogs wore raincoats! Then July 4 was (**3.** cold) than an icicle in January. The next day the air became (**4.** warm), and it started to rain cats and dogs. Nothing could have been (**5.** silly). The (**6.** funny) thing was a puddle full of wet poodles.

Then something even (**7.** strange) happened. The weird weather just stopped, and the sun came out. Now the people of Lightning Flats are (**8.** busy) than ever trying to figure out where all those cats and dogs went.

Spell Chat

Challenge a classmate to name two more pairs of words that have **-er** and **-est** endings.

B Word Study: Synonyms

Write a spelling word that is a synonym for each word or phrase.

9. more amusing
10. soonest
11. most foolish
12. easier
13. damper
14. chilliest
15. gloomiest
16. sooner
17. more unhappy
18. most active
19. hottest
20. easiest

C Write

Write a flyer for a class play. Use these words.

funniest   altogether

_____

_____

Spelling Words

busier	colder
busiest	coldest
earlier	stranger
earliest	strangest
funnier	simpler
funniest	simplest LOOKOUT WORD
sillier	wetter
silliest	wettest
warmer	sadder
warmest	saddest

Review	Challenge
altogether	fiercer
cheated	loveliest
silly	

My Words

_____

_____

_____

_____

Spelling Words

busier	colder
busiest	coldest
earlier	stranger
earliest	strangest
funnier	simpler
funniest	simplest
sillier	wetter
silliest	wettest
warmer	sadder
warmest	saddest

Review	Challenge
altogether	fiercer
cheated	loveliest
silly	

My Words

Quick Write

Write a sentence or two about something you did last weekend. Use at least two spelling words.

You may wish to do this activity on a computer.

A Write a Journal Entry

Imagine that you are visiting an imaginary place. Tell about it in a journal entry. Who is there? What do you do? How do you like it there? Use four spelling words.

B Proofread

Mike wrote a journal entry about the imaginary Planet Zona. He made three spelling errors, one punctuation error, and one mistake in subject-verb agreement. Help him correct his errors.

Tip
Subjects and verbs must agree in person and in number.

This cloudy gray planet is the strangest place I've ever seen. It is warmer and weter than our home on Earth. The fourth graders in school here are much busyer than we are, too. They wears the funniest clothes, but they are very friendly. Alltogethr, I'm having fun and learning a lot. Every night my robot helps me with my homework

PROOFREADING MARKS

∧ Add
⊙ Add a period
ℓ Take out
↻ Move
≡ Capital letter
/ Small letter
¶ Indent paragraph

Now proofread your journal entry. Check spelling, punctuation, and subject-verb agreement.

Study and Review

Ⓐ Use the Dictionary: Guide Words

The guide words at the top of a dictionary page tell you the first and last entry word on the page. All the entries listed between the guide words are in alphabetical order. Here is an example of guide words on a dictionary page.

code ▶ coleslaw

Which spelling words would you find between the guide words *code* and *coleslaw*?

_____   _____

Write the spelling words that belong on a dictionary page with these guide words.

burr•but _____

ear•ease _____

strain•stream _____

Ⓑ Test Yourself

Add the ending to each base word. Remember, some words have a spelling change when *-er* and *-est* are added. Write the spelling word.

1. simple + er
2. silly + est
3. strange + er
4. busy + er
5. sad + est
6. funny + er
7. wet + est
8. warm + est
9. early + er
10. cold + est
11. simple + est
12. silly + er
13. strange + est
14. busy + est
15. sad + er
16. funny + est
17. wet + er
18. warm + er
19. early + est
20. cold + er

For Tomorrow...
Get ready to share the words with **-er** and **-est** that you discovered, and remember to study for your test!

Word Study Strategy

See the word

START

Say it slowly

Link sounds and letters

Write

Check

END

Spelling Words

elf	shelf
elves	shelves
half	wife
halves	wives
leaf	wolf
leaves	wolves
life	knife
lives	knives
loaf	yourself
loaves	yourselves

LOOKOUT WORD

Review	Challenge
simplest	scarf
damaged	scarves
geese	

My Words

_____

_____

_____

_____

Plurals

A See and Say

The Spelling Concept

shelf	shelves
life	lives

To make a noun that ends in the letters *f* or *fe* plural, change *f* or *fe* to *ve* and add *s*.

> One furry wolf
> Seven wolves

MEMORY JOGGER

B Link Sounds and Letters

Say each spelling word. Listen for the ending sound. Notice the spelling for the plural form of the word. Then sort the words on a chart like this one.

Word Sort

Singular Noun ends in *f* or *fe*	Plural Noun ends in *ves*

C Write and Check

Read the brain teaser. Write the spelling word that is in it.

_____

BRAIN TEASER

Why are playing cards like wolves?

They both come in a pack!

A Build Vocabulary: **Classifying**

Write the spelling word that belongs in each group.

1. stem, flower, ___
2. drawer, bin, ___
3. husband, child, ___
4. herself, myself, ___
5. dog, fox, ___
6. quarter, third, ___
7. spoon, fork, ___
8. troll, giant, ___
9. birth, death, ___
10. roll, bun, ___
11. children, husbands, ___

Spell Chat

Ask a classmate to say and spell the **plural** of *calf.* Then check the spelling in a dictionary.

B Word Study: **Word Clues**

Write the plural that fits each clue.

12. These turn color and fall in the autumn.
13. These doglike animals run in packs.
14. You can buy these in a bread bakery.
15. These tools are used for cutting.
16. Two of these make a whole.
17. You can store dishes on these.
18. Biographies are the stories of these.
19. This pronoun refers to you and your friends.
20. These characters sometimes appear in legends and fairy tales.

C Write

Write the first two sentences of a fairy tale. Use these words:

elves   half   simplest

_____

_____

Be a Spelling Sleuth

Look in folktales and fantasies to find nouns that end in f, fe, or ves. For example, *elf, loaves,* and *wolves.* List the words you find.

Spelling Words

elf	shelf
elves	shelves
half	wife
halves	wives
leaf	wolf
leaves	wolves
life	knife
lives	knives
loaf	yourself
loaves	yourselves

LOOKOUT WORD

Review	Challenge
simplest	scarf
damaged	scarves
geese	

My Words

_____

_____

_____

_____

Spelling Words

elf	shelf
elves	shelves
half	wife
halves	wives
leaf	wolf
leaves	wolves
life	knife
lives	knives
loaf	yourself
loaves	yourselves

LOOKOUT WORD

Review	Challenge
simplest	scarf
damaged	scarves
geese	

My Words

Quick Write

Write titles for two legends or folktales. Use three spelling words.

You may wish to do this activity on a computer.

A Write a Legend

Create a legend that explains something that happens in nature. For example, you might tell why we have rain and thunder or why birds fly south in the winter. Use at least four spelling words.

B Proofread

Michelle wrote a legend about fall. She made three spelling errors, one capitalization error, and one punctuation error. She also used an article incorrectly. Correct her errors.

Tip

Always use the article *a* before a word that begins with a consonant sound. Use the article *an* before a word that begins with a vowel sound.

> *How Fall Came to the Forest*
>
> Long ago a farmer lived in a Forest. He raised gese and was a friend to the trees. One cold fall day, a angry pack of wolfs chased him away The trees wept and shed their leaves. The branches remained bare until the farmer returned the next spring. That is why trees lose their leafs in the autumn.

Now proofread your legend. Check for spelling, punctuation, and correct use of articles.

PROOFREADING MARKS

∧ Add
⊙ Add a period
ℓ Take out
◯∧ Move
≡ Capital letter
／ Small letter
¢ Indent paragraph

Ⓐ Use the Dictionary: Idioms

An idiom is a phrase or expression that means something different from what it seems to mean. Sometimes idioms are found in dictionary entries. Read the entry for *wolf*.

> **with ▶ wonder**
>
> **wolf** /wŏŏlf/
>
> 1. *noun* A wild animal that looks like a dog. 2. *idiom* To **cry wolf** means to give a false alarm to get attention.

Write a sentence, using the idiom for *wolf*.

_____

Look in the Spelling Dictionary under the word *leaf*. Write the idiom in the entry and tell what it means.

_____

_____

Ⓑ Test Yourself

Write the singular form of the spelling word that fits the clue. Then write the plural form.

1–2. animal that howls

3–4. one of two parts

5–6. not *myself*, but ___

7–8. part of a plant

9–10. the time between birth and death

11–12. a married woman

13–14. a ___ of bread

15–16. an imaginary creature

17–18. tool to cut with

19–20. part of a bookcase

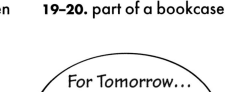

For Tomorrow...
Get ready to share the **plurals** you found in folktales and fantasies. Remember to study for your test!

Get Word Wise

The word *loaf* comes from the Old English word *hlaf*, which meant "food" or "bread." Long ago, *hlaf* or bread was often the main food people ate. Over time, the meaning of *loaf* changed. Today it names not only bread but also any food that has the shape of a loaf of bread, such as meatloaf.

Word Study Strategy

See the word

START

Say it slowly

Link sounds and letters

Write

Check

END

Spelling Words

chief
grief
thief
relief
belief
believe
receive
either
neither
field

fierce
weigh
freight
neighbor
height
ceiling
diet *LOOKOUT WORD*
soldier
niece
review

Review	Challenge
yourselves	sleigh
cried	shield
friend	

My Words

Words With ie or ei

A See and Say

The Spelling Concept

believe   ceiling   freight   height

The letters *ie* and *ei* can stand for /ē/ as in *believe and ceiling*.
The letters *ei* can also stand for /ā/ as in *freight* and
/ī/ as in *height*.

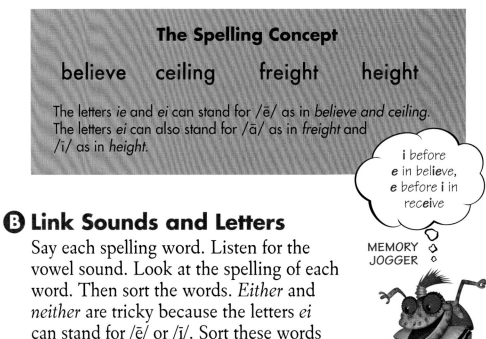

i before
e in believe,
e before i in
receive

MEMORY JOGGER

B Link Sounds and Letters

Say each spelling word. Listen for the
vowel sound. Look at the spelling of each
word. Then sort the words. *Either* and
neither are tricky because the letters *ei*
can stand for /ē/ or /ī/. Sort these words
according to the way *you* say them.

Word Sort

/ā/ spelled ei	/ē/ spelled ie	/ē/ spelled ei	/ī/ spelled ei	Other Words

C Write and Check

Read the word puzzle and follow
the directions. You will write three
spelling words.

WORD PUZZLE

Write relief.
Change r to b.
Change f to ve.

_____

_____

_____

Vocabulary Practice

Ⓐ Build Vocabulary: Antonyms

Write the spelling word that means the opposite.

1. not nephew, but _____

2. not give, but _____

3. not floor, but _____

4. not happiness, but _____

5. not neither, but _____

6. not disbelief, but _____

7. not tame, but _____

Spell Chat

Use an antonym in a sentence to say the opposite of what you mean. For example, *My neighbor's dog is very tame.* Ask a classmate to figure out what you really mean to say.

Ⓑ Word Study: Analogies

Complete each analogy with a spelling word.

8. *Play* is to *replay*, as *view* is to _____.

9. *Friend* is to *pal*, as *leader* is to _____.

10. *Or* is to *either*, as *nor* is to _____.

11. *Car* is to *automobile*, as *load* is to _____.

12. *Ounce* is to *weight*, as *inch* is to _____.

13. *Loaves* is to *loaf*, as *thieves* is to _____.

14. *Strawberry* is to *patch*, as *corn* is to _____.

15. *Team* is to *player*, as *army* is to _____.

16. *Clothing* is to *clothes*, as *food* is to _____.

17. *Measured* is to *measure*, as *weighed* is to _____.

Ⓒ Write

Write a short e-mail message you might send to a friend. Use these words.

neighbor   believe   relief

_____

_____

_____

Be a Spelling Sleuth

Look in newspapers and neighborhood newsletters to find words with *ie* or *ei*. For example, *field, neighbor,* or *ceiling.* Keep a list.

Spelling Words

chief	fierce
grief	weigh
thief	freight
relief	neighbor
belief	height
believe	ceiling
receive	diet LOOKOUT WORD
either	soldier
neither	niece
field	review

Review	Challenge
yourselves	sleigh
cried	shield
friend	

My Words

_____

_____

_____

_____

You may wish to do this activity on a computer.

Spelling Words

chief	fierce
grief	weigh
thief	freight
relief	neighbor
belief	height
believe	ceiling
receive	diet *LOOKOUT WORD*
either	soldier
neither	niece
field	review

Review	Challenge
yourselves	sleigh
cried	shield
friend	

My Words

Quick Write

Describe a food. Tell how it looks and tastes, but don't tell its name. See if a partner can identify the food from your description. Use two spelling words.

A Write Your Observations

Recall an outdoor area you have visited. Write observations about the place in your nature log. For example, if you found an interesting pine cone, you could write about its size, texture, shape, and color. Use three spelling words.

B Proofread

Casey recorded his observations about a storm. He made five spelling errors and one punctuation error. He also needed to combine two sentences to make a compound predicate. Help Casey correct his errors.

Tip
You can combine two sentences that have the same subject and make one sentence with a compound predicate.

On our field trip, my frend Mia and I found a clump of cattails Their hieght was over six feet. Suddenly it began to get dark. Overhead black clouds rolled across the sky. Black clouds threw shadows over everything. They were stratus clouds. They looked like a sealing over the feild. What a releif it was to get into our school bus.

PROOFREADING MARKS

∧ Add
⊙ Add a period
ℓ Take out
◠ Move
≡ Capital letter
/ Small letter
¶ Indent paragraph

Now proofread your observations. Check spelling and punctuation, and look for sentences that you can combine.

Ⓐ Use the Dictionary: Example Sentence

A dictionary entry often includes an example sentence. An example sentence can help you better understand the meaning of an entry word and how it is used. Read the entry for *fierce*. Notice the example sentence for each meaning.

> **fierce** /fērs/ *adjective*
> **1.** Violent or dangerous. *A lion is a fierce animal.* **2.** Very strong or extreme. *The fierce wind blew down many trees.*

Write another example sentence for each meaning of *fierce*.

_____

_____

Look up the word *relief* in your Spelling Dictionary. Write an example sentence for each meaning.

_____

_____

Ⓑ Test Yourself

Use the code to write each spelling word.

 # = ie   *** = ei**

1. bel#f	**6.** bel#ve	**11.** sold#r	**16.** c*ling
2. *ther	**7.** fr*ght	**12.** w*gh	**17.** rel#f
3. n*ghbor	**8.** gr#f	**13.** rec*ve	**18.** f#rce
4. d#t	**9.** n*ther	**14.** rev#w	**19.** h*ght
5. ch#f	**10.** f#ld	**15.** n#ce	**20.** th#f

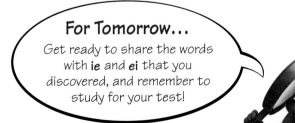

For Tomorrow... Get ready to share the words with **ie** and **ei** that you discovered, and remember to study for your test!

Get Word Wise

Neighbor comes from an Anglo-Saxon word that meant "a boor who lives nigh, or nearby." Today *boor* means "a rude person," but in the old days, *boor* meant "farmer." So a *neighbor* was just the person who lived on the next farm.

Word Study Strategy

START

See the word

Say it slowly

Link sounds and letters

Write

Check

END

Star Dreams

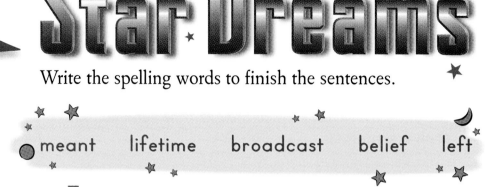

Write the spelling words to finish the sentences.

meant   lifetime   broadcast   belief   left

Three, two, one, liftoff! As the spacecraft Endeavour (1) the launching pad at the Kennedy Space Center on September 12, 1992, Dr. Mae Jemison became the first African-American woman in space. It was the thrill of a (2) . Aboard the spacecraft, she thought about what the trip (3) to her. In a TV (4) from space she said, "I'm closer to the stars— somewhere I've always dreamed to be!" It had taken many steps to get there, but Jemison always held the (5) that her dream would come true.

receive   taught   brought   life   earlier

Even as a child, Mae Jemison always wanted to be an astronaut. She (6) herself everything she could about space. After college, she became a doctor. However, she never forgot her dream from an (7) time in her (8) . She was accepted into NASA's astronaut program in 1987. She had taken a giant step, one that (9) her much closer to her goal. She finally began to (10) training to be an astronaut.

sleep   busier   runway   yourself   hardware

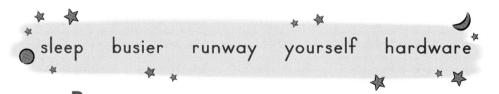

Dr. Jemison learned how to deal with the lack of gravity in space— how to handle floating tools and (11) and how to (12) standing up. She was (13) than ever during training. Five years later, she got her chance to go into space. After 127 orbits of Earth, the Endeavour and its crew landed on the (14) at the Kennedy Space Center on September 20. You might say that Dr. Mae Jemison's motto is: Believe in (15) and follow your dreams.

Word Building

Read the word clues for compound words. Choose a word from each box to form the compound word.

1. a large juicy fruit _____
2. a memory about the past _____
3. the landing of a spacecraft in the ocean _____
4. a small cleaning tool _____
5. stiff paper _____
6. the rays of the sun from dawn to evening _____
7. what remains when everything else is used _____
8. a small book with a soft cover _____

day
tooth
water
card
splash
flash
paper
left

brush
back
down
light
melon
over
board

Context Clues

either	strangest	leave	bought	slept
believe	catch	neighbor	earlier	left

Write the spelling word that completes the sentence.

9. Benita woke up and looked at the clock. "Oh, no," she cried, "I've _____ late!"

10. "I should have gotten up _____."

11. "Now, I'll never _____ the school bus."

12. "It will probably _____ without me."

13. She dressed, ate, and _____ the house.

14. Outside there wasn't a _____ in sight.

15. There were no little children playing, _____.

16. Where was everybody? It was the _____ thing.

17. She looked at the watch with the day and date that she had _____ recently.

18. "I don't _____ it," she said. "It's Saturday!"

Double Compounds

Write the word that is the end of one compound word and the beginning of another. For example, paper**back**pack.

splash_____town

note_____case

left_____sleep

life_____table

day_____house

believe
bring
colder
earlier
build
funnier
funniest
half
left

life
lifetime
lives
sleep
teach
warmer
weigh
wolves
yourself

Tip
Remember to
capitalize proper
nouns.

On the Move

Write one or two sentences for a travel guide about each of the following places. Your goal is to make the place sound interesting and fun. Use two spelling words in each description.

1. Museum of American History

_____

_____

2. Weatherstone National Park

_____

_____

3. Cartoonville, USA

_____

_____

4. Washington, D.C.

_____

_____

5. Planet Z

_____

_____

Look back at My Words and the words you misspelled in your Unit 5 Posttests. Use them in another description.

6. Alottafun Amusement Park

_____

_____

Listen to This!

Use five spelling words to write a radio ad for one of the places you described above. Proofread it for spelling, capitalization, and punctuation. Then read it to a partner.

Weigh Your Words!

Have you ever heard this spelling rule? Write *i* before *e* except after *c*, and except when the sound is long *a* as in *neighbor* and *weigh*. Write the *ie* or *ei* word that fits each clue. Use the spelling rule if you need help.

> ceiling   review   neighbor   soldier   believe
> weigh   niece   chief   fierce   field   receive

1. the head of a group _____

2. to get something _____

3. a baseball diamond _____

4. a synonym for *wild* _____

5. the part of a room that is opposite the floor _____

6. aunt and uncle, _____ and nephew

7. to think that something is true _____

8. a man or woman in the army _____

9. to find out how heavy a thing is _____

10. someone who lives nearby _____

11. to study something again _____

> either   neither   height

Here are some words that are exceptions to the spelling rule. How can you remember the exceptions? You just have to memorize them.

12. I'm sorry _____ Julio nor Marta can go with us.

13. Your _____ is how tall you are.

14. We'll have _____ turkey or chicken.

Eileen says...

I wrote about a special event in my journal. Here's what I said: "My uncle is a train engineer. As a special treat, he let me ride with him in the engine of a fright train that was 47 cars long!"

My teacher wrote back a note saying, "That must have been scary!" I couldn't figure out what she meant, until I realized that I had written *fright train* instead of *freight train*. One letter can change the meaning of a word totally. It's frightening!

Spelling Matters!

Suffix -y

Ⓐ See and Say

The Spelling Concept

cloud	cloudy
noise	noisy
mud	muddy

Many words become adjectives when -y is added to the base word. Sometimes the spelling of the base word changes before adding -y.

Spelling Words

angry	muddy
breezy	noisy
bumpy	rainy
chewy	sandy
cloudy	shiny
creepy	sleepy
curly	slippery
gloomy	sunny
hungry	thirsty
lumpy	windy

LOOKOUT WORD

Review	Challenge
diet	wintry
forgiven	quirky
party	

My Words

_____

_____

_____

_____

*Look for the **slipper** in **slipper**y.*

MEMORY JOGGER

Ⓑ Link Sounds and Letters

Say each spelling word. Listen for the suffix -y. Look at the base word and notice whether or not the spelling changes when -y is added. Then sort the spelling words on a chart like this one.

Word Sort

No Change	Drop Final e	Double the Final Consonant	Other Words

Ⓒ Write and Check

Read this tongue twister aloud. Say it as quickly as you can. Then write the spelling word in the tongue twister.

_____

TONGUE TWISTER

Six sleek sleds slide on slick, slippery slopes.

A Build Vocabulary: Add a Suffix

Write the adjective that completes each sentence. Add the suffix *-y* to each base word in ( ). Remember that sometimes the spelling of the base word changes before *-y* is added.

1. I still felt (sleep) when I woke up today.

2. Outside the weather was cold and (rain).

3. The smell of food made me (hunger).

4. I ran to the kitchen and ate a (chew) bagel.

5. I was (thirst) so I drank some juice.

6. Maybe it's a good day to see a (creep) movie.

7. We can't roller skate because the streets are (slip).

8. The ground is too (mud) to ride our bikes.

9. I guess I like clear (sun) days better.

Spell Chat

Challenge the person next to you to use three of the spelling words in a phrase. For example, *a muddy, bumpy, slippery road.*

B Word Study: Word Clues

Write the spelling word that goes with each clue.

10-11. They rhyme with *grumpy*.

12. It begins with *w* and has short *i*.

13. It means the same thing as *mad*.

14. It means the opposite of *dull*.

15. Its base word rhymes with *sneeze*.

16. The small word *and* is in its middle.

17. It rhymes with *roomy*.

18. It means the same thing as *loud*.

19. It means the opposite of *straight*.

20. It begins like *clever* and ends like *ready*.

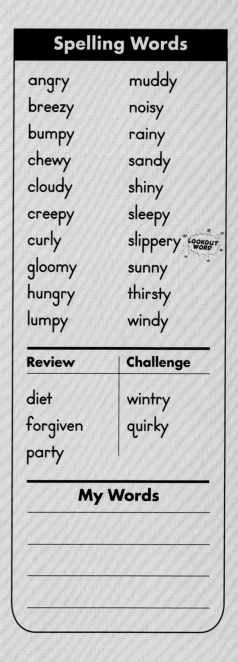

Be a Spelling Sleuth

Each day this week, check weather forecasts on radio, TV, and in the newspapers. Keep a list of words to which the suffix -y has been added. For example, *rainy, snowy, windy.*

Spelling Words

angry	muddy
breezy	noisy
bumpy	rainy
chewy	sandy
cloudy	shiny
creepy	sleepy
curly	slippery LOOKOUT WORD
gloomy	sunny
hungry	thirsty
lumpy	windy

Review	Challenge
diet	wintry
forgiven	quirky
party	

My Words

You may wish to do this activity on a computer.

Spelling Words

angry	muddy
breezy	noisy
bumpy	rainy
chewy	sandy
cloudy	shiny
creepy	sleepy
curly	slippery
gloomy	sunny
hungry	thirsty
lumpy	windy

LOOKOUT WORD

Review	Challenge
diet	wintry
forgiven	quirky
party	

My Words

A Write a Biographical Sketch

Think of someone you know well. It might be a friend or a family member. What does that person look like, and what does he or she do? Write a sketch that describes the person. Use four spelling words.

B Proofread

Pedro wrote this sketch about his favorite aunt. He made three spelling errors, two capitalization errors, and one error in punctuation. Correct them.

Tip
Don't forget to capitalize people's names and titles, such as Dr. Jane Yamamoto or Uncle Bob.

> You should meet my aunt Rosa! She is very kind. In fact, I've never seen her angery. Aunt Rosa acts in movies and lives in sunny California. She is tall and has brown curly hair Last summer we went to a great partey at her house. We spent the evening on the sandie beach. A mariachi band led by mr. Perez played Mexican folk songs, and Aunt Rosa even danced for us.

PROOFREADING MARKS
∧ Add
⊙ Add a period
ℓ Take out
○∧ Move
≡ Capital letter
/ Small letter
¶ Indent paragraph

Quick Write

Write two interview questions you might ask a person you admire. Use two spelling words.

Now proofread your biographical sketch. Check for spelling, punctuation, and capitalization.

Ⓐ Use a Thesaurus: **Synonyms**

A thesaurus is a reference book that lists synonyms for an entry word. Sometimes a thesaurus also lists antonyms. You can use a thesaurus to give your writing variety. A thesaurus can also help you find exactly the right word to use. Read the thesaurus entry for *gloomy*.

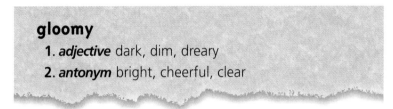

> **gloomy**
> 1. *adjective* dark, dim, dreary
> 2. *antonym* bright, cheerful, clear

Rewrite the sentence. Use a synonym for the underlined word.

In California, we rarely have <u>gloomy</u> days.

_____

Use an antonym for *gloomy* in a sentence.

_____

Ⓑ Test Yourself

Complete each spelling word by adding the missing vowels and the suffix -*y*.

1. r_ _ n_
2. s_nn_
3. c_rl_
4. br_ _ z_
5. gl_ _ m_
6. th_rst_
7. ch_w_
8. m_dd_
9. w_nd_
10. sh_n_
11. sl_ _ p_
12. _ngr_
13. sl_pp_r_
14. cr_ _ p_
15. l_mp_
16. n_ _ s_
17. b_mp_
18. s_nd_
19. h_ngr_
20. cl_ _ d_

For Tomorrow...
Get ready to share words with the suffix -**y** that you collected, and remember to study for your test!

Word Study Strategy

START

See the word

Say it slowly

Link sounds and letters

Write

Check

END

Spelling Words

unable
unbeaten
uncommon
unfinished
unhappy
unkind
unknown
unlucky
unusual
unwrap

disagree
disappear
disappoint
disconnect
discourage
discover
dishonest
dislike
disobey *LOOKOUT WORD*
nonsense

Review	Challenge
slippery	unfortunate
taught	nonstop
finish	

My Words

_____

_____

_____

Prefixes un-, dis-, non-

A See and Say

The Spelling Concept

Prefix	Meaning	Example
un-	not	unkind
dis-	the opposite of	dishonest
non-	not	nonsense

A prefix is a word part added to the beginning of a word. The meaning of a base word can change when a prefix is added. The prefixes *un-*, *dis-*, and *non-* usually mean "not." Adding one of these prefixes to a word makes that word mean the opposite.

They never disobey.

MEMORY JOGGER

B Link Sounds and Letters

Say each spelling word. Listen for the prefixes *un-*, *dis-*, and *non-*. Sort the spelling words in a chart like this one.

Word Sort

Prefix *un-*	Prefix *dis-*	Prefix *non-*

C Write and Check

Write the spelling words in the riddle.

_____

_____

RIDDLE

Why was the little horse unhappy?

Every time it asked for something, its mother would disagree and say, "Neigh."

Vocabulary Practice

Ⓐ Build Vocabulary: Word Families

The words *unbeaten*, *unbeatable*, and *beaten* all belong to the same family. They each have *beat* as a base word. Write the spelling word that belongs to each word family.

1. wrapper, rewrap, ___

2. connects, reconnect, ___

3. happiness, happiest, ___

4. finishes, refinish, ___

5. sense, sensible, ___

6. covering, recover, ___

7. kindness, unkindly, ___

8. encourage, courage, ___

9. reappear, appears, ___

10. appoints, reappoint, ___

Ⓑ Word Study: Prefixes

The prefix *un-*, *dis-*, or *non-* was left off each underlined word below. Add the correct prefix, and make the sentence mean the opposite of what it says.

11. The Traveling Tooters are a very <u>common</u> type of band.

12. The drummers <u>like</u> loud music.

13. They all <u>obey</u> the band leader.

14. The band members always <u>agree</u> about which songs to learn.

15. They are <u>beaten</u> in every competition.

16. The <u>lucky</u> band marched in our Labor Day parade.

17. The sick trumpet player was <u>able</u> to toot his horn.

18. The band had to play the most <u>usual</u> songs.

19. Most of the pieces were <u>known</u> to everyone.

20. It would be <u>honest</u> to say that the Traveling Tooters were a big hit.

Spell Chat

Ask a classmate to build other word families that have words with the prefixes **un-** or **dis-**.

Spelling Words

unable	disagree
unbeaten	disappear
uncommon	disappoint
unfinished	disconnect
unhappy	discourage
unkind	discover
unknown	dishonest
unlucky	dislike
unusual	disobey *LOOKOUT WORD*
unwrap	nonsense

Review	Challenge
slippery	unfortunate
taught	nonstop
finish	

My Words

_____

_____

_____

_____

Spelling Words

unable	disagree
unbeaten	disappear
uncommon	disappoint
unfinished	disconnect
unhappy	discourage
unkind	discover
unknown	dishonest
unlucky	dislike
unusual	disobey *LOOKOUT WORD*
unwrap	nonsense

Review	Challenge
slippery	unfortunate
taught	nonstop
finish	

My Words

Quick Write

Write an ad for a play about a folktale or fable. Use at least three spelling words.

You may wish to do this activity on a computer.

Write and Proofread

Ⓐ Write a Fable

A fable is a story that teaches a lesson. Write a fable set in an interesting or unusual place. Use at least four spelling words and other words with *un-*, *dis-*, and *non-*.

Ⓑ Proofread

Sarah wrote a fable set in the Southwest. She made three spelling errors, one punctuation error, and one capitalization error. She also used one linking verb incorrectly. Correct her errors.

Tip

Make sure that linking verbs—*am, is, are, was,* and *were*—agree with the subject.

> Rabbit and Crow
> All summer Rabbit and Crow gathered food for winter. They worked as a team. It was uncommon to hear them disagre. "We won't rest until we finich our work," they said. their neighbor Coyote played while they worked and made unkinde remarks about them. Soon the winter snows came. Rabbit and Crow was warm and well fed. Outside, unhappy Coyote howled

Now proofread your fable. Check for spelling, punctuation, and the correct use of linking verbs.

PROOFREADING MARKS

∧ Add
⊙ Add a period
ℓ Take out
↻ Move
≡ Capital letter
/ Small letter
¢ Indent paragraph

Study and Review

A Use the Dictionary: Multiple Meanings

The dictionary lists different meanings for a word and numbers them. Here is a dictionary entry for *disagree*.

> **dis•a•gree** /dis ə grē/ *verb*
> 1. To have a different opinion from someone else.
> 2. To cause discomfort. *Peppers disagree with me.*
> ▶ disagreeing, disagreed

Which meaning does *disagree* have in each sentence? Write the number.

_____ Roberto dislikes strawberries because they disagree with him.

_____ Will Erica disagree with our movie choice?

Look up the word *discover* in the Spelling Dictionary. Write a sentence for each meaning.

_____

_____

B Test Yourself

Figure out the prefix that goes with each spelling word. Write the word.

1. __wrap	8. __beaten	15. __common
2. __like	9. __kind	16. __cover
3. __sense	10. __courage	17. __agree
4. __finished	11. __connect	18. __happy
5. __usual	12. __obey	19. __appear
6. __honest	13. __able	20. __lucky
7. __appoint	14. __known	

For Tomorrow...
Get ready to share words with the prefixes **un-**, **dis-**, and **non-** that you discovered, and remember to study for the test.

Get Word Wise
The word *courage* comes from an Old French word that meant "heart." Long ago, people thought that a brave person was someone who had a large heart. Even today you may hear the expression "She has plenty of heart" to describe someone who is particularly courageous and not easily discouraged.

Word Study Strategy

See the word

START

Say it slowly

Link sounds and letters

Write

Check

END

Spelling Words

beautiful (LOOKOUT WORD)	helpless
careful	thankful
careless	thankless
harmful	thoughtful
harmless	thoughtless
colorful	useful
colorless	useless
fearful	wonderful
fearless	worthless
helpful	priceless

Review	Challenge
disobey	skillful
headache	restless
awful	

My Words

Suffixes -ful and -less

A See and Say

The Spelling Concept

beautiful	full of beauty
harmful	able to harm
fearless	without fear
priceless	unable to be priced

A suffix is a word part added to the end of a word. The meaning of a base word can change when a suffix is added. The suffix *-ful* means "full of " or "able to." The suffix *-less* means "without," "not having," or "unable to."

Change the y to i in beauty to make it beautiful.

MEMORY JOGGER

B Link Sounds and Letters

Say each spelling word. Listen for the base word and suffix. Sort the words on a chart like this one.

Word Sort

-ful	-less

C Write and Check

A small word is missing from each word. Read the clues in the puzzle to figure out each small word. Then write the complete spelling word.

_____

_____

_____

PUZZLE

a body part
h _ _ _ ful

frozen water
pr _ _ _ less

a cob of corn
f _ _ _ ful

A Build Vocabulary: **Antonyms**

Look at the underlined word in each phrase. Then write the antonym that has the same base word. For example, the antonym of *harmless* is *harmful.*

1. a <u>fearful</u> person
2. a <u>colorful</u> kite
3. a <u>thankless</u> worker
4. a <u>useful</u> machine
5. a <u>thankful</u> gesture
6. a <u>thoughtless</u> friend
7. a <u>fearless</u> puppy
8. a <u>thoughtful</u> speech
9. a <u>colorless</u> painting
10. a <u>useless</u> idea

Spell Chat
Challenge the person next to you to think of other pairs of opposites with the suffix **-ful** or **-less**, such as *restful* and *restless*. Be sure each is a real word.

B Word Study: **Word Clues**

Write the spelling word with the suffix *-ful* or *-less* that means the same as each clue.

11. taking care
12. without care
13. able to help
14. not having help
15. unable to be priced
16. able to produce wonder
17. not having worth
18. able to harm
19. unable to harm
20. full of beauty

C Write

Write a Help Wanted ad for a job in a glass factory. Use these spelling words.

careful   beautiful   priceless   colorful

_____

_____

_____

Spelling Words

beautiful LOOKOUT WORD	helpless
careful	thankful
careless	thankless
harmful	thoughtful
harmless	thoughtless
colorful	useful
colorless	useless
fearful	wonderful
fearless	worthless
helpful	priceless

Review	Challenge
disobey	skillful
headache	restless
awful	

My Words

_____

_____

_____

_____

Spelling Words

beautiful *LOOKOUT WORD*	helpless
careful	thankful
careless	thankless
harmful	thoughtful
harmless	thoughtless
colorful	useful
colorless	useless
fearful	wonderful
fearless	worthless
helpful	priceless

Review	Challenge
disobey	skillful
headache	restless
awful	

My Words

_____

_____

_____

_____

Quick Write

Write a headline for a news event that might happen in the future. Use at least two spelling words.

You may wish to do this activity on a computer.

A Write a News Story

Think about an unusual event that might happen in the year 2010. It might be a new kind of transportation or a new city built on a space station. Imagine that you are a reporter. Write about the event. Include four spelling words.

Tip

Place a comma between the day and year when writing a date, as in January 1, 2000.

B Proofread

Luther wrote this news story about an imaginary event in the future. He made four spelling errors, one capitalization error, and one punctuation error. Correct them.

> July 4 2010 was truly a wonderfull day for two hundred families. After three months of aweful travel by spaceship, they arrived at their new home on Space Station 5. The fearles travelers were thankful to have finally reached this beutifull space age city of two million people. One boy said, "this is the most awesome place in space!"

PROOFREADING MARKS

∧ Add
⊙ Add a period
ℓ Take out
↶↷ Move
≡ Capital letter
／ Small letter
¶ Indent paragraph

Now proofread your news story. Check for spelling, punctuation, and capitalization.

Ⓐ Use the Dictionary: Word History

Many dictionaries give a separate word history for certain words. A word history often traces the word back to its earliest forms and meanings. It may include changes the word has undergone along the way.

> ### Word History
> The word **care** comes to us from the Old German word *chara* that meant "to show sadness." Sometime before the year 1000 A.D., the suffix *-ful* was added to make the word *careful*. People of that time used *careful* to mean "troubled" or "worried." Over the years the meaning of *careful* changed. Today, if you are careful, you do something thoughtfully and don't take any risks.

Which language has given us the word *care*?

_____

What did the word *careful* once mean?

_____

Ⓑ Test Yourself

Write the spelling word that rhymes with each made-up word. The rhymes may not have the same spelling.

1. farmful
2. charmless
3. blankful
4. crankless
5. tootieful
6. shareful
7. bareless
8. boughtful
9. foughtless
10. underful
11. steerful
12. nearless
13. museful
14. fuseless
15. earthless
16. dullerful
17. dullerless
18. kelpful
19. yelpless
20. sliceless

For Tomorrow...
Get ready to share the words with suffixes **-ful** and **-less** you discovered, and remember to study for the test!

Get Word Wise
The base word *fear* in *fearful* comes from an Old English word that meant "sudden danger." As time passed, people began to use the word *fear* to describe the feelings that a person has when he or she is in danger.

Word Study Strategy

See the word

START

Say it slowly

Link sounds and letters

Write

Check

END

Spelling Words

awfully
eagerly
easily
gently
gladly
happily
lately
lonely
luckily
mostly

only   LOOKOUT WORD
partly
really
sadly
simply
slowly
strangely
truly
quickly
quietly

Review	Challenge
beautiful	ordinarily
strangest	clumsily
early	

My Words

Suffix -ly

Ⓐ See and Say

The Spelling Concept

quick	+ ly	quickly
easy	+ ly	easily
gentle	+ ly	gently

Some adverbs and adjectives end with the suffix -ly. Sometimes there is a spelling change when -ly is added to a base word.

I did it easily.

MEMORY JOGGER

Ⓑ Link Sounds and Letters

Say each spelling word. Listen for the -ly suffix. Look for the base word. Notice how the spelling of some base words changes when -ly is added. Sort the spelling words on a chart like this one.

Word Sort			
No Change to Base Word	Drop e or le	Change y to i	Other Words

Ⓒ Write and Check

Read the joke. Write the two words that are spelling words.

_____

_____

JOKE

Why did the little boy eagerly take the butter on an airplane?

He really wanted to see butter fly. (butterfly)

Ⓐ Build Vocabulary: Using Adverbs

An adverb describes a verb. It may tell how, when, where, how often, or how much something happens. Add *-ly* to the word in ( ) to make the adverb that completes each sentence. Write the adverb.

1. Last week, I (eager) read a folktale about Anansi the Spider.

2. I thought the story was (awful) funny.

3. In it, Anansi was acting (strange).

4. He (quick) tricked a friend into doing all the work.

5. I have also enjoyed other African folktales (late).

6. I (happy) found a book by Julius Lester called *How Many Spots Does Leopard Have?*

7. It is (easy) one of the best collections around.

8. I (simple) can't wait to read his other books.

Spell Chat

Challenge a classmate to think of two more adverbs that end in *-ly* and use each in a sentence.

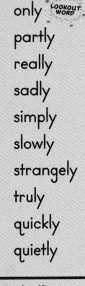

Ⓑ Word Study: Suffixes

Do the word math to make a base word. Then add the suffix *-ly*. Write the spelling word. Remember that the spelling of some base words changes when *-ly* is added.

9. mad − m + s
10. bad − b + gl
11. ducky − d + l
12. blue − bl + tr
13. bone − b + l
14. grow − gr + sl
15. post − p + m
16. cart − c + p
17. seal − s + r
18. gerbil − rbil + ntle

Ⓒ Write

Write tips for giving a surprise party. Use these words.

only   quietly   early

_____

_____

Be a Spelling Sleuth

Look for words ending in -ly in books and stories you read. For example, *playfully, hourly, instantly, eagerly*. Make a list of the words you find.

Spelling Words

awfully	only
eagerly	partly
easily	really
gently	sadly
gladly	simply
happily	slowly
lately	strangely
lonely	truly
luckily	quickly
mostly	quietly

Review	Challenge
beautiful	ordinarily
strangest	clumsily
early	

My Words

_____

_____

_____

_____

Spelling Words

awfully	only
eagerly	partly
easily	really
gently	sadly
gladly	simply
happily	slowly
lately	strangely
lonely	truly
luckily	quickly
mostly	quietly

Review	Challenge
beautiful	ordinarily
strangest	clumsily
early	

My Words

Quick Write

Write two sentences to introduce an important person who is speaking to your class. Use three spelling words.

You may wish to do this activity on a computer.

Ⓐ Write Interview Questions

Think of a person who has a job you might like to do someday. What would you ask that person about his or her job? Write six questions. Use four spelling words.

Ⓑ Proofread

Michelle wrote these interview questions for TV star LeVar Burton. She made four spelling errors, one punctuation error, and one capitalization error. Correct the errors.

> **Tip**
> Begin a question with a capital letter and end it with a question mark.

1. How earley does your workday begin?

2. How quickly can you shoot one episode of a TV show

3. What kinds of shows are truly your favorites?

4. why did you realy decide to become an actor?

5. What part of your job do you do most easyly?

6. What projects have you been working on latly?

PROOFREADING MARKS

∧ Add
⊙ Add a period
ℓ Take out
↻ Move
≡ Capital letter
/ Small letter
¶ Indent paragraph

Now proofread your interview questions. Check for spelling, punctuation, and capitalization.

Ⓐ Use the Dictionary: Pronunciation

Each entry word in a dictionary is followed by a respelling that shows you how to pronounce the word. A pronunciation key tells you what the symbols in the pronunciation mean. Here's an entry word and part of a pronunciation key.

luck•y /luk ē/

ā	**a**ce	ī	**i**ce
ä	p**a**lm	ō	**o**pen
ē	**e**qual	u	**u**p
i	**i**t	yōō	f**u**se
		ə	nick**e**l

Write the spelling word that goes with each pronunciation.

/mōst lē/ _____   /ōn lē/ _____

/pärt lē/ _____   /lāt lē/ _____

/lōn lē/ _____   /byōō ti fəl/ _____

/sim plē/ _____   /kwik lē/ _____

Ⓑ Test Yourself

Use the code to figure out your spelling words. Write each word.

△ = a   * = e   # = i   % = o $ = u   □ = ly

1. % n □
2. s △ d □
3. * △ s # □
4. t r $ □
5. h △ p p # □
6. m % s t □
7. s t r △ n g * □

8. △ w f $ l □
9. * △ g * r □
10. s l % w □
11. g * n t □
12. r * △ l □
13. q $ # * t □
14. l $ c k # □

15. s # m p □
16. l △ t * □
17. g l △ d □
18. q $ # c k □
19. l % n * □
20. p △ r t □

For Tomorrow...
Get ready to share the words with -ly, and remember to study for your test.

Get Word Wise

The base word *strange* in *strangely* comes from a Latin word that meant "outside." At one time, something outside the town's walls was "strange," or unknown. Over time, *strange* took on the meaning we use today— odd or different.

Word Study Strategy

START
See the word
Say it slowly
Link sounds and letters
Write
Check
END

Word Building

A See and Say

Spelling Words

cheerful

cheerfully

fairly

unfairly

needless

needlessly

hopeful

hopefully

hopeless

hopelessly

playful

playfully

faithful

faithfully

delightful

delightfully

peaceful

peacefully

tireless

tirelessly

LOOKOUT
WORD

Review	Challenge
only	unpleasantly
wolves	disrespectfully
care	

My Words

The Spelling Concept

hope	hopeful	hopefully
fair	unfair	unfairly

Sometimes more than one prefix or suffix can be added to a base word to build new words.

See the **light** in de**light**ful.

MEMORY
JOGGER

B Link Sounds and Letters

Say each spelling word. Listen for the base word. Ask yourself: Does the word have a prefix? Does it have one or more suffixes? Sort the spelling words by writing each word in the correct column.

Word Sort

Words With Prefixes	Words With One Suffix	Words With Two Suffixes

C Write and Check

Write the three spelling words in the rhyme.

_____

_____

_____

HAY DAY

The tireless farmer
Hopped on his tractor,
But bailing the hay
Was hopeless that day.
Why? It's needless to say —
The tractor was tireless!

Ⓐ Build Vocabulary: **Word Meaning**

Write the spelling word that completes each sentence.

1. A person who wishes for the best is ___.

2. To play according to the rules is to play ___.

3. Something that is unnecessary is ___.

4. A puppy that is full of fun is ___.

5. A classmate that is joyful and glad is ___.

6. A worker who requires little rest is ___.

7. A loyal friend is ___.

8. Something that is sure to disappoint is ___.

9. A movie that is funny and pleasing is ___.

10. A calm and quiet place is very ___.

Spell Chat

Challenge the person next to you to add **prefixes** and/or **suffixes** to *care* and *fear* and to use the new words in sentences.

Be a Spelling Sleuth
Read about people who make news. Make a list of words that have one or more prefixes or suffixes. For example, *skillful, gracefully,* and *delightful.* Keep a list.

Ⓑ Word Study: **Word Families**

Complete each word-family pyramid with a spelling word. Add a suffix to the last word in each pyramid.

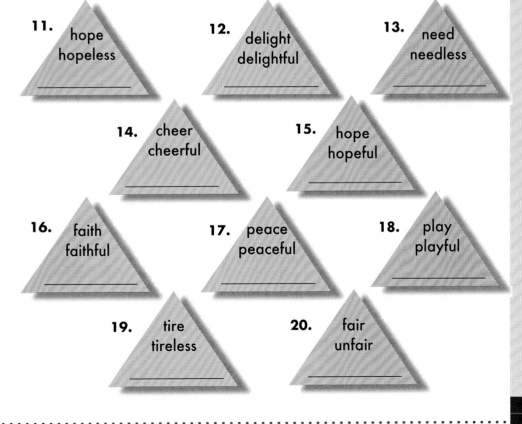

11. hope
hopeless
____

12. delight
delightful
____

13. need
needless
____

14. cheer
cheerful
____

15. hope
hopeful
____

16. faith
faithful
____

17. peace
peaceful
____

18. play
playful
____

19. tire
tireless
____

20. fair
unfair
____

Spelling Words

cheerful	playful
cheerfully	playfully
fairly	faithful
unfairly	faithfully
needless	delightful
needlessly	delightfully
hopeful	peaceful
hopefully	peacefully
hopeless	tireless
hopelessly	tirelessly

Review	Challenge
only	unpleasantly
wolves	disrespectfully
care	

My Words
____
____
____
____
____

Spelling Words

cheerful	playful
cheerfully	playfully
fairly	faithful
unfairly	faithfully
needless	delightful
needlessly	delightfully
hopeful	peaceful
hopefully	peacefully
hopeless	tireless
hopelessly	tirelessly

LOOKOUT WORD

Review	Challenge
only	unpleasantly
wolves	disrespectfully
care	

My Words

Quick Write

Write a short two-sentence review of a nonfiction story you have read. Use at least two spelling words.

You may wish to write your story on a computer.

Ⓐ Write a Nonfiction Story

Think of a recent event. It may have been national news or something that happened in your community. Write the beginning of the story about the event. Use four spelling words.

Spelling Tip

Remember that irregular past-tense verbs such as ran, knew, and thought are not formed by adding -ed.

Ⓑ Proofread

Carlos wrote the beginning of a nonfiction story about a dog walk. He made four spelling errors, one punctuation error, and wrote one irregular verb incorrectly.

Gina Wong was hopeful that the Paws-for-Pets March would be a success. Owners and their playfull pooches strutted chearfuly in Payne's Park to raise money for the city's ownly dog shelter. Gina knowed that she had worked tirelessly on this event. Needles to say, she and her faithful dog Max were right in the middle of all those wagging tails

PROOFREADING MARKS

∧ Add
⊙ Add a period
ℓ Take out
○↗ Move
≡ Capital letter
／ Small letter
¶ Indent paragraph

Now proofread the beginning of your nonfiction story. Check for spelling, punctuation, and correct verb tenses.

Study and Review

A Use the Dictionary: Accented Syllables

In a dictionary, the accented syllable is often shown in boldface letters in the word's pronunciation. In some dictionaries, an accent mark (´) is used. Read the following words, and listen for the accented syllable.

cheer·ful /**chēr** fəl/	**faith·ful** /**fāth** fəl/
un·fair /un **fâr**/	**de·light·ful** /di **līt** fəl/
need·less /**nēd** lis/	**hope·less** /**hōp** lis/

Write the words in which the first syllable is accented. Circle the base words.

_____   _____

_____   _____

Write the words in which the second syllable is accented. Circle the base words.

_____   _____

Did you notice that the base word is accented when prefixes and suffixes are added?

B Test Yourself

Put the syllables in order and write each spelling word.

1. fulplay
2. lyfair
3. lesshope
4. fuldelightly
5. fulfaith
6. lessneed
7. fulcheerly
8. fulhope
9. lylesstire
10. fulpeacely
11. fulcheer
12. lesslyhope
13. lyfairun
14. fulplayly
15. lessneedly
16. fulpeace
17. fullyfaith
18. lesstire
19. fuldelight
20. lyfulhope

For Tomorrow...
Get ready to share words with **prefixes** and **suffixes** that you discovered, and remember to study for the test!

Get Word Wise

Did you ever playfully pretend that you were asleep to fool a friend? If so, you "played possum." This idiom comes from the behavior of the possum, a gray, furry, woodland animal. When possums are threatened by an enemy, they pretend they are asleep or dead. For possums, this is a defense, not a playful action.

Word Study Strategy

See the word

START

Say it slowly

Link sounds and letters

Write

Check

END

Rescue Patrol

Write the spelling words to complete the story.

cloudy   discover   hopefully
playful   unlucky

On a cold, (1) day last week I was having a (2) game of tag with my friend Lisa. Suddenly we received an urgent phone call from the forest service. We had a job. Two (3) campers were lost in the mountains, and we needed to find them. We would (4) them before dark, (5).

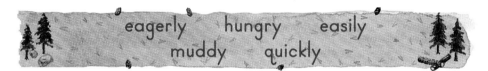

eagerly   hungry   easily
muddy   quickly

Lisa hurried to pack her medical kit and some food, in case the lost people were (6). She (7) carried everything to the truck, and we drove to the trailhead where the people were last seen. The trail was wet and (8), but I brushed off my nose and started sniffing. I found their scent quite (9), with no trouble at all. "This way," I barked (10).

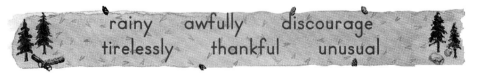

rainy   awfully   discourage
tirelessly   thankful   unusual

The weather turned (11), but it didn't stop or (12) us. Half way up the mountain I heard a high, (13) sound in the distance and turned off the trail. Lisa followed me steadily and (14). We hiked another mile before we found the campers. "We're (15) glad to see you!" they yelled. Lisa patted my head and smiled. "Just be (16) that Max is a such a good rescue dog," she said proudly.

Antonyms

worthless
beautiful
noisy
cheerful
curly
fearless
shiny
useful

Make each phrase mean the opposite of what it says. Write the spelling word that is an antonym for each underlined word.

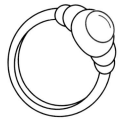

1. a <u>dull</u> gold ring _____

2. an <u>ugly</u> black coat _____

3. very <u>straight</u> hair _____

4. a <u>grumpy</u> character _____

5. a <u>useless</u> present _____

6. a <u>quiet</u> city street _____

7. a <u>valuable</u> painting _____

8. a <u>frightened</u> superhero _____

Word Meanings

bumpy
gloomy
lonely
thirsty
unfinished
colorless
delightful
faithful
disappoint

Write the spelling word that fits each clue.

9. A loyal and trustworthy person is _____.

10. To let friends down is to _____ them.

11. Something that isn't completed is _____.

12. A _____ person needs a drink of water.

13. Something that pleases you a lot is _____.

14. A clear piece of glass is _____.

15. Something that is dark and dull is _____.

16. A road that is not smooth and even is _____.

17. Someone who wants company may feel _____.

Alphabet Code

Use an alphabet code to solve the riddle. Find the letter in the alphabet that comes two letters before the given letter. For example, for **d** you would write **b**.

f g n k i j v h w n

What did the candle say to the lamp?

You're _ _ _ _ _ _ _ _ _ _!

In the News

Read each headline. Write the first two sentences of the news story that follows it. Use at least three spelling words in the sentences.

disappear
easily
faithfully
happily
hopeful
hungry
only
priceless
really
thoughtful
tireless
unbeaten
wonderful

Tip
Make sure you make any necessary spelling changes to base words when you add suffixes.

PROOFREADING MARKS

∧ Add
⊙ Add a period
ℓ Take out
↷ Move
≡ Capital letter
/ Small letter
¶ Indent paragraph

1. Lander Tigers Score Five Easy Wins and No Losses

_____

_____

2. Fourth Graders Pack Food Baskets for Picnic

_____

_____

3. Wet Weather May Vanish by Weekend

_____

_____

4. Fourth Graders Create Fish Mural for School

_____

_____

5. Girl Finds Valuable Fossil in Quiet Field

_____

_____

Look back at My Words and the words you misspelled in your Unit 6 Posttests. Use them to write another opening for a news story.

6. Firefighter Rescues Kitten

_____

_____

Question Time

You want to interview a person who appears in one of the stories above. Write five questions you might ask. Proofread your questions for spelling, capitalization, and punctuation. Try your questions out on a partner.

Totally Suffixes

The suffixes *-y*, *-ful*, *-less*, and *-ly* can be added to nouns and verbs to make adjectives and adverbs. Write the word with a suffix that completes each sentence.

peaceful   peacefully   useful   useless

1. We pitched our tent by the _____ stream.

2. We were so tired that we slept _____.

3. This flat bicycle tire is _____.

4. It is _____ to carry a tire pump on a long ride.

··· happily   hopeful   muddy   sadly ···

5. We _____ watched the funny new movie.

6. We are _____ that the next one will be good, too.

7. Our morning soccer game ended _____. We lost.

8. Now the field is too wet and _____ to play.

··· noisy   playful   playfully   quietly ···

9. I _____ closed the window and went to bed.

10. Much later, a _____ truck zoomed by and woke me up.

11. The yellow cat _____ chased the ball.

12. The _____ young dog caught it in mid-air.

Margaret says...

I wrote a letter to my piano teacher and signed it, "Yours truely, Margaret." When he wrote back, I noticed that he signed the letter, "Yours truly" and left out the e in *truly*.

I didn't know which spelling was correct. I checked the dictionary and learned that you drop the e when you add *-ly* to *true*. Now I'm truly careful when I write a letter.

Spelling Matters!

Handwriting Models

A B C D E F G H I
J K L M N O P Q R
S T U V W X Y Z
a b c d e f g h i j
k l m n o p q r s t
u v w x y z

A B C D E F G H I
J K L M N O P Q R
S T U V W X Y Z
a b c d e f g h i j
k l m n o p q r s t
u v w x y z

already	decided	instead	piece	thirsty
altogether	dinner	knew	pleasant	thorough
beautiful	dollar	know	please	though
belief	double	lead	puzzle	thought
believe	doubt	lesson	quarter	threw
board	dough	letter	quiet	through
bough	drawer	little	quit	throughout
bought	dropped	middle	quite	thumb
breakfast	either	mountain	really	tiny
buy	enough	neighbor	receive	tough
calendar	family	neither	remember	trouble
captain	favorite	nickel	review	truly
caught	field	niece	rough	unusual
choose	fierce	notice	route	vacation
chose	follow	off	shiny	weather
colorful	fossil	often	square	weigh
cough	found	only	squirrel	weight
country	half	peace	summer	whistle
course	health	people	surprise	wrote
cousin	height	picture	temperature	yourself

You will find all your spelling words in alphabetical order in the Spelling Dictionary. Look at the sample entry below to see how to find information about the words you look up.

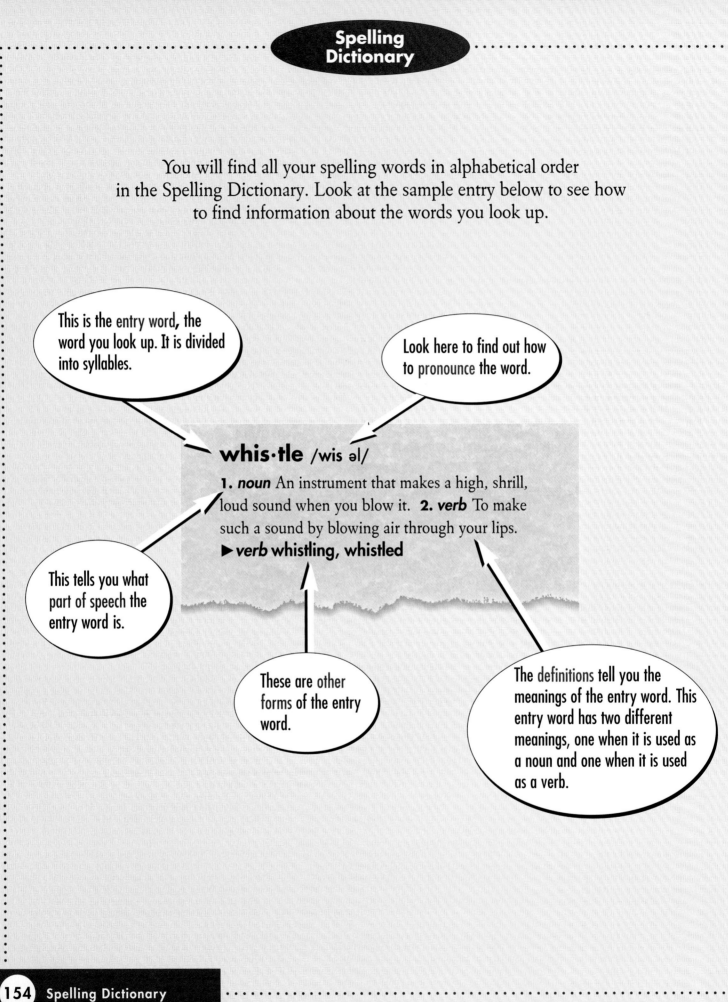

This is the entry word, the word you look up. It is divided into syllables.

Look here to find out how to pronounce the word.

whis·tle /wis əl/

1. noun An instrument that makes a high, shrill, loud sound when you blow it. **2. verb** To make such a sound by blowing air through your lips.
▶**verb** whistling, whistled

This tells you what part of speech the entry word is.

These are other forms of the entry word.

The definitions tell you the meanings of the entry word. This entry word has two different meanings, one when it is used as a noun and one when it is used as a verb.

A a

a·ble /ā bəl/ *adjective*
1. Capable; can do something.
2. Skillful or talented.

ac·count /ə kount/
1. *noun* A description of something that happened. 2. *noun* An arrangement to keep money in a bank. 3. *verb* To explain is to *account for* it. ▶**accounting, accounted**

ad·ven·ture /ad ven chər/
noun An exciting experience.

af·ter /af tər/ *preposition*
1. Later than, as in *after lunch*.
2. Following behind. *The puppy ran after me.*

a·head /ə hed/ *adverb*
1. In front. 2. In the future.

al·lowed /ə loud/ *verb*
Let someone do something. Past tense of **allow**. **Allowed** sounds like **aloud**.

a·loud /ə loud/ *adverb*
In a voice that others can hear. **Aloud** sounds like **allowed**.

al·read·y /ôl red ē/ *adverb*
Before now.

al·to·geth·er /ôl tə geth ər/
adverb 1. In total. 2. Completely; entirely.

a·mount /ə mount/ *noun*
How much there is of something.

an·gry /ang grē/ *adjective*
Feeling or showing anger.

an·nounce /ə nouns/ *verb*
To say something officially or publicly.

ap·plaud·ed /ə plôd əd/ *verb*
Showed that you liked something by clapping your hands. Past tense of **applaud**.

ap·ple /ap əl/ *noun*
A round, crisp fruit with a red, yellow, or green skin.

as·tound·ing /ə stound ing/
adjective Very surprising; amazing.

aw·ful·ly /ô fəl lē/ *adverb*
1. Terribly. 2. Very.

B b

bare /bâr/
1. *adjective* Without covering.
2. *adjective* Empty. 3. *verb* To uncover or reveal something. **Bare** sounds like **bear**.

bas·ket /bas kit/ *noun*
A container, often with handles, made of cane, wire, or other material woven together.

bear /bâr/
1. *verb* To support or carry something. 2. *noun* A large, heavy animal with thick fur. **Bear** sounds like **bare**.

beau·ti·ful /byōō ti fəl/ *adjective*
Very pleasant to look at or listen to.

be·lief /bi lēf/ *noun*
Something held to be true.

be·lieve /bi lēv/ *verb*
1. To feel sure that something is true. **2.** To support someone or something. ▶ **believing, believed**

bet·ter /bet ər/ *adjective*
1. More suitable, or higher in quality. **2.** No longer ill or hurting.

bil·lion /bil yən/ *noun*
One thousand times one million (1,000,000,000).

bliz·zard /bliz ərd/ *noun*
A heavy snowstorm.

board /bôrd/
1. *noun* A flat piece of wood. **2.** *verb* To get on a train, an airplane, and so on. **Board** sounds like **bored**.

bored /bôrd/ *verb*
Found a thing or person very dull and not interesting. **Bored** sounds like **board**.

bor·ough /bur ō/ *noun*
A town or village. **Borough** sounds like **burrow**.

bor·row /bor ō/ *verb*
To use something that belongs to someone else, with the understanding that it will be returned.

bot·tle /bot əl/
1. *noun* A glass or plastic container that holds a liquid. **2.** *verb* To put things into bottles.

bot·tom /bot əm/ *noun*
The lowest part.

bough /bou/ *noun* A thick branch on a tree.

bought /bôt/ *verb*
Purchased something with money. Past tense of **buy**.

bounce /bouns/ *verb*
To spring back after hitting something.

bread /bred/ *noun*
A baked food made from flour, water, and often yeast.

break·fast /brek fəst/ *noun*
The first meal of the day.

Word History

Breakfast refers to the fact that this meal breaks the fast, the period during the night when no food is eaten.

breez·y /brē zē/ *adjective*
Having light winds blowing.

bring /bring/ *verb*
1. To take something or someone to a place.
2. To make something happen or appear. *Clouds often bring rain.* **3.** **bring up** To look after and guide a child as he or she grows up. ▶ **bringing, brought**

broad·cast /brôd kast/
1. *verb* To send out a program on television or radio.
2. *noun* A television or radio program.

broke /brōk/ *verb*
Damaged something so that it is in pieces and no longer works. Past tense of **break**.

bro·ken /brō kən/ *verb* Damaged.

brought /brôt/ *verb*
Took something or someone to a place. Past tense of **bring**.

bub·ble /bu bəl/
1. *noun* One of the tiny balls of gas in fizzy drinks, boiling water, and so on. 2. *verb* To make bubbles. *The boiling water bubbled.* ▶ *verb* **bubbling, bubbled**

buf·fa·lo /buf ə lō/ *noun*
1. A type of ox with heavy horns found in Europe, Africa, and Asia. 2. A bison.

build /bild/ *verb*
To make something by putting different parts together. ▶ **building, built**

built /bilt/ *verb*
Made something by putting different parts together. Past tense of **build**.

bum·ble·bee /bum bəl bē/
noun A large, hairy bee with yellow and black stripes.

bump·y /bum pē/ *adjective* Very uneven.

bur·ied /ber ēd/ *verb*
1. Put something underground. 2. Covered up or hid.

bur·row /bur ō/
1. *noun* A tunnel in the ground made or used by an animal. 2. *verb* To dig or live in such a tunnel. **Burrow** sounds like **borough**.

bur·y·ing /ber ē ing/ *verb*
1. Putting something underground. 2. Covering up or hiding.

bus·i·er /biz ē ər/ *adjective*
Having more things to do; more active.

bus·i·est /biz ē ist/ *adjective* Most active.

but·ton /but ən/ *noun*
1. A round piece of plastic or metal on clothing and used as a fastener. 2. A knob that you turn or press to make a machine work.

buy /bī/ *verb*
To get something by paying money for it.
▶ **buying, bought**

buzz /buz/ *verb*
To make a noise like a bee or wasp.

C c

cab·in /kab in/ *noun*
1. A small, simple house, often built of wood.
2. A private room to sleep in on a ship.

cal·en·dar /kal ən dər/ *noun*
A chart showing all the days, weeks, and months in a year.

calf /kaf/ *noun*
1. A young cow, seal, elephant, giraffe, or whale.
2. The fleshy part at the back of your leg, below your knee. ▶ *plural* **calves**

cap·tain /kap tən/ *noun*
1. The person in charge of a ship or an aircraft.
2. The leader of a sports team. 3. An officer in the armed forces.

a	add	ô	order	th	this
ā	ace	o͞o	took	zh	vision
â	care	o͞o	pool		
ä	palm	u	up		
e	end	û	burn	ə	=
ē	equal	yo͞o	fuse	a	in *above*
i	it	oi	oil	e	in *sicken*
ī	ice	ou	pout	i	in *possible*
o	odd	ng	ring	o	in *melon*
ō	open	th	thin	u	in *circus*

cap·ture /kap chər/ *verb*
1. To take a person, an animal, or a place by force.
2. To attract and hold. *She captured my attention.*

card·board /kärd bôrd/ *noun*
Thick, stiff material for making boxes.

care·ful /kâr fəl/ *adjective*
Paying close attention to do something well or to avoid mistakes or injuries.

care·less /kâr ləs/ *adjective*
Not paying close attention to a task being done; often making mistakes.

cas·tle /kas əl/ *noun*
A large ancient building, often with a wall and moat.

catch /kach/
1. *verb* To grab hold of something moving through the air, as in *to catch a ball*. 2. *verb* To get something or someone you are chasing. 3. *noun* A game in which two or more people throw a ball to one another.
▶ *verb* catches, catching, caught

cat·er·pil·lar /kat ər pil ər/ *noun*
A larva that changes into a butterfly or moth.

caught /kôt/ *verb*
Grabbed hold of something moving through the air. Past tense of **catch**.

cau·tion /kô shən/
1. *noun* Carefulness or watchfulness. 2. *verb* To warn.

ceil·ing /sē ling/ *noun*
The upper surface of a room, opposite the floor.

cel·lar /sel ər/ *noun*
A room below ground level in a house, often used for storage. **Cellar** sounds like **seller**.

cer·tain /sûr tən/ *adjective*
1. Sure of something. 2. Particular.

chap·ter /chap tər/ *noun*
1. One of the parts into which a book is divided.
2. A branch of an organization.

chat·ted /chat əd/ *verb*
Talked. Past tense of **chat**.

chat·ter /chat ər/ *verb*
To talk about unimportant things.

chat·ting /chat ing/ *verb* Talking.

cheat·ed /chēt əd/ *verb* Acted dishonestly. Past tense of **cheat**.

cheat·ing /chēt ing/ *verb* Acting dishonestly.

check·ers /chek ərz/ *noun*
A board game for two players.

cheer·ful /chēr fəl/ *adjective* Happy.

cheer·ful·ly /chēr fə lē/ *adverb* Happily.

cheese /chēz/ *noun*
A food made from the solid parts of milk.

chews /chōōz/ *verb*
Grinds food between the teeth. **Chews** sounds like **choose**.

chew·y /chōō ē/ *adjective*
Needing much chewing, such as *a chewy piece of meat*.

chief /chēf/
1. *noun* The leader of a group of people. 2. *adjective* Main, or most important.

choose /chōōz/ *verb*
To pick out one thing from several. **Choose** sounds like **chews**. ▶choosing, chose, chosen

chose /chōz/ *verb* Picked. Past tense of **choose**.

climb /klīm/
1. *verb* To move upward. **2.** *noun* An upward movement or slope.

cloud·y /kloud ē/ *adjective*
1. Covered with clouds. **2.** Not clear.

clum·si·ly /klum zə lē/ *adverb*
In a careless, awkward manner.

coarse /kôrs/ *adjective*
Having a rough texture or surface. **Coarse** sounds like **course**.

cold·er /kōld er/ *adjective*
Having a lower temperature; chillier.

cold·est /kōld ist/ *adjective*
Having the lowest temperature; chilliest.

col·lar /kol ər/ *noun*
1. The part of a shirt, blouse, or coat that fits around your neck. **2.** A thin band of material worn around the neck of a pet.

col·or·ful /kul ər fəl/ *adjective*
1. Full of color. **2.** Having variety; interesting.

col·or·less /kul ər lis/ *adjective*
1. Without color. **2.** Uninteresting; dull.

comb /kōm/
1. *noun* A flat piece of metal or plastic with teeth, used for making hair neat. **2.** *verb* To use a comb. **3.** *verb* To search a place thoroughly.
▶ *verb* combing, combed

con·clu·sion
/kən klōō zhən/ *noun*
1. The final part; end. **2.** A decision or realization based on the facts.

con·di·tion /kən dish ən/
1. *noun* The general state of a person, an animal, or a thing. **2.** *verb* To get into good health. *Exercise conditions your body.* **3.** *noun* A medical problem that continues over a long period of time as in a *heart condition*.

con·fusion /kən fyōō zhən/ *noun*
1. A state of disorder. **2.** A mistaking of one thing or person for another.

cop·ied /kop ēd/ *verb*
1. Did the same as someone else. **2.** Made a copy of something. Past tense of **copy**. ▶ copy, copies, copying

cop·y·ing /kop ē ing/ *verb*
1. Doing the same as someone else. **2.** Making a copy of something.

cot·ton /kot ən/ *noun*
1. A cloth made from the fluffy white fibers surrounding the seed pods of a certain plant. **2.** The plant that produces such fibers.

cough /kôf/
1. *verb* To make a sudden, harsh noise as you force air out of your lungs. **2.** *noun* An illness that makes you cough.

a	add	ô	order	th	this
ā	ace	ōō	took	zh	vision
â	care	ōō	pool		
ä	palm	u	up		
e	end	û	burn	ə	=
ē	equal	yōō	fuse	a	in *above*
i	it	oi	oil	e	in *sicken*
ī	ice	ou	pout	i	in *possible*
o	odd	ng	ring	o	in *melon*
ō	open	th	thin	u	in *circus*

count /kount/ *verb*
1. To say numbers in order. **2.** To work out how many there are of something. **3.** To be worth something. *Your opinion counts.*

coun·try /kun trē/ *noun*
1. A part of the world with its own borders and government. **2.** Land away from towns and cities.

coun·ty /koun tē/ *noun*
A division or part of a state with its own local government.

course /kôrs/ *noun*
1. A part of a meal served by itself. **2.** A series of lessons. **3.** An area where a sport is played. **Course** sounds like **coarse**.

cou·sin /kuz ən/ *noun*
The child of one's aunt or uncle.

crack·er /krak ər/ *noun*
A thin, plain biscuit or wafer.

cra·zy /krā zē/ *adjective*
Insane or foolish.

crea·ture /krē chər/ *noun* A living being.

creep /krēp/ *verb*
1. To move very slowly and quietly. **2.** To crawl.
▶ **creeping, crept**

creep·y /krē pē/ *adjective*
Having or giving a feeling of horror or fright.

crept /krept/ *verb*
Moved slowly and quietly. Past tense of **creep**.

cried /krīd/ *verb*
1. Wept. **2.** Shouted out. Past tense of **cry**.

crowd /kroud/
1. *noun* Many people packed together. **2.** *verb* To fill by pressing or thronging together. The passengers *crowd* into the full bus.

crumb /krum/ *noun*
A tiny piece of bread or cake.

crum·ble /krum bəl/ *verb*
To break into small pieces. ▶ **crumbling, crumbled**

cry·ing /krī ing/ *verb* Weeping.

cul·ture /kul chər/ *noun*
The way of life, ideas, customs, and traditions of a group of people.

cur·ly /kûr lē/ *adjective* Having curls.

 D d

dam·aged /dam ijd/ *verb*
Harmed. Past tense of **damage**.

dam·ag·ing /dam ij ing/ *verb*
Harming.

day·light /dā līt/ *noun*
The light of the sun during daytime hours.

de·cid·ed /di sīd əd/ *verb*
Made up one's mind. Past tense of **decide**.

de·cid·ing /di sīd ing/ *verb*
Making up one's mind about something.

de·ci·sion /di sizh ən/ *noun*
The act of making up one's mind; a choice or judgment made about something.

de·light·ful /di līt fəl/ *adjective*
Giving great pleasure.

de·light·ful·ly /di līt fəl lē/ *adverb*
In a pleasing manner.

de·liv·er /di liv ər/ *verb*
1. To take something to someone. 2. To say, as in *deliver a speech*.

de·nied /di nīd/ *verb*
1. Said something that is not true. 2. Stopped someone from having something or from going somewhere. *The guard denied us entry to the closed building.* ▶deny, denies, denying

de·ny·ing /di nī ing/ *verb*
Saying that something is not true.

de·vel·op·ing /di vel əp ing/ *verb*
1. Growing 2. Building on something. *She is developing her skills as a painter.* 3. Treating film with chemicals to bring out the pictures.

di·et /dī ət/
1. *noun* What a person usually eats. 2. *noun* A selected eating plan. 3. *verb* To choose what you eat in order to lose weight, gain weight, or improve your health.

di·ner /dīn ər/ *noun*
1. A person eating in a restaurant. 2. A restaurant with a long counter and small booths.

din·ner /din ər/ *noun*
1. The main meal of the day. 2. A formal banquet.

dis·a·gree /dis ə grē/ *verb*
1. To have a different opinion from someone else. 2. To cause discomfort. *Peppers disagree with me.*

dis·ap·pear /dis ə pir/ *verb*
To go out of sight.

dis·ap·point /dis ə point/ *verb*
To let someone down.

dis·con·nect /dis kə nekt/ *verb*
To separate things that are joined together.

dis·cour·age /dis kûr ij/ *verb*
To try to prevent someone from doing something.

dis·cov·er /dis kuv ər/ *verb*
1. To find something. 2. To find out about something.

dis·cus·sion /dis kush ən/ *noun*
A talk about an issue that includes different points of view.

dis·ease /də zēz/ *noun* An illness.

dis·hon·est /dis on ist/ *adjective*
Not honest or fair.

dis·like /dis līk/ *verb*
To have a feeling of displeasure about a person or thing. ▶disliking, disliked

dis·o·bey /dis ə bā/ *verb*
To go against the rules or someone's wishes.

dis·res·pect·ful·ly /dis ri spekt fəl lē/ *adverb* In a manner showing no respect.

di·vid·ed /də vīd əd/ *verb*
Split into parts. Past tense of **divide**.

di·vid·ing /də vīd ing/ *verb*
Splitting into parts.

a	add	ô	order	th	this
ā	ace	o͞o	took	zh	vision
â	care	o͞o	pool		
ä	palm	u	up		
e	end	û	burn	ə	=
ē	equal	yo͞o	fuse	a	in *above*
i	it	oi	oil	e	in *sicken*
ī	ice	ou	pout	i	in *possible*
o	odd	ng	ring	o	in *melon*
ō	open	th	thin	u	in *circus*

di·vi·sion /di vizh ən/ *noun*
1. Dividing one number by another. 2. One of the parts into which something large has been divided.

dol·lar /dol ər/ *noun*
1. 100 cents, the main unit of money in the United States. 2. A similar unit of money in certain other countries, such as Canada and Australia.

dol·phin /dol fin/ *noun*
An intelligent water mammal with a long snout, related to a whale but smaller.

dou·ble /du bəl/
1. *adjective* Twice the amount. 2. *adverb* Twice as much. 3. *verb* To make something twice as big.

doubt /dout/
1. *noun* Uncertainty. 2. *verb* To question or disbelieve something.

dough /dō/ *noun*
A thick, sticky mixture used to make bread, cookies, and other foods. **Dough** sounds like **doe**.

down·town /doun toun/ *adverb*
To or in a city's main business district.

draw·er /drôr/ *noun*
A sliding box in a piece of furniture, used for storage.

drawn /drôn/ *verb*
1. To have made a picture. 2. To have pulled something. ▶ **draw, drawing, drew**

drew /drōō/ *verb*
1. Made a picture. 2. Pulled something. Past tense of **draw**.

dri·ven /driv ən/ *verb*
To have gone in a car or other vehicle. ▶ **drive, driving, drove**

drooped /drōōpt/ *verb*
Hung down. Past tense of **droop**.

droop·ing /drōōp ing/ *verb* Hanging down.

dropped /dropt/ *verb*
1. Let fall down. 2. Fell down. Past tense of **drop**.

drop·ping /drop ing/ *verb* Falling down.

drought /drout/ *noun*
A long period of very dry weather.

drove /drōv/ *verb*
Went in a car or other vehicle. Past tense of **drive**.

drow·sy /drou zē/ *adjective* Sleepy.

E e

ea·ger /ē gər/ *adjective*
Very interested in doing something; enthusiastic.

ea·ger·ly /ē gər lē/ *adverb*
With great interest and feeling.

ear·li·er /ûr lē ər/ *adjective*
Before something else or someone else.

ear·li·est /ûr lē ist/ *adjective*
The first one, before anyone or anything else.

earth·quake /ûrth kwāk/ *noun*
A sudden, violent shaking of the earth.

eas·i·ly /ē zə lē/ *adverb* In an easy way.

eaves·drop /ēvz drop/ *verb*
To listen in secret to someone's conversation.
▶ **eavesdropping, eavesdropped**

Word History

Eavesdrop comes from the Old English word *yfesdrype*. Eaves are the lower edge of a roof. If people happened to stand under the eaves, they might overhear what people inside were saying.

ei·ther /ē thər or ī thər/
1. *conjunction* Indicates a choice. **2.** *pronoun* One of two. **3.** *adverb* Also; similarly.

el·e·phant /el ə fənt/ *noun*
A large animal with a long trunk; may also have ivory tusks.

el·e·va·tor /el ə vā tər/ *noun*
A machine that carries people or goods up and down among different floors or levels of a building.

elf /elf/ *noun*
A small, mischievous, make-believe character described in fairy tales.

elves /elvz/ *noun*
Characters in fairy tales. Plural of **elf**.

em·ptied /emp tēd/ *verb*
Took the contents out of a container. Past tense of **empty**.

em·pty·ing /emp tē ing/ *verb*
Taking the contents out of a container.

e·nough /i nuf/ *adjective*
As much as is needed.

e·qual·i·ty /i kwol ə tē/ *noun*
The same rights for everyone.

e·ven /ē vən/ *adjective*
1. Flat and smooth. **2.** Can be divided exactly by two, as in *an even number*. **3.** Equal, as in *an even score*.

ex·plo·ra·tion /eks plə rā shən/ *noun*
The act of looking into or studying something or someplace new.

fact /fakt/ *noun*
A piece of information that is true.

faint /fānt/
1. *adjective* Not clear or strong. **2.** *adjective* Dizzy; weak. **3.** *verb* To become dizzy and unconscious.

fair·ly /fâr lē/ *adverb*
1. In a fair or equal manner. **2.** Moderately.

faith·ful /fāth ful/ *adjective* Loyal.

faith·ful·ly /fāth fəl lē/ *adverb*
Showing loyalty.

fam·i·ly /fam ə lē/ *noun*
A group of people related to one another.

fan·tas·tic /fan tas tik/ *adjective*
1. Too strange to be believable. **2.** Terrific.

a	add	ô	order	th	this
ā	ace	o͝o	took	zh	vision
â	care	o͞o	pool		
ä	palm	u	up		
e	end	û	burn	ə	=
ē	equal	yo͞o	fuse	a	in *above*
i	it	oi	oil	e	in *sicken*
ī	ice	ou	pout	i	in *possible*
o	odd	ng	ring	o	in *melon*
ō	open	th	thin	u	in *circus*

fash·ion /fash ən/
1. *noun* A style of clothing that is popular at a certain time. **2.** *verb* To make or shape something.

fa·vor /fā vər/
1. *noun* A kind deed. **2.** *verb* To like one thing or person best.

fa·vor·ite /fā və rit/ *noun*
1. The person or thing someone likes best.
2. The person, team, or animal expected to win.

fear·ful /fir fəl/ *adjective* Full of fear.

fear·less /fir lis/ *adjective* Very brave.

feast /fēst/ *noun* A large, fancy meal.

feath·er /feth ər/ *noun*
One of the light, fluffy parts that cover a bird's body.

fea·ture /fē chər/ *noun*
Part of the face, such as the eyes, nose, mouth, or chin.

fel·low /fel ō/
1. *noun* A man or boy. **2.** *adjective* Belonging to the same group.

fe·ver /fē vər/ *noun*
A body temperature that is higher than normal (98.6°F).

fic·tion /fik shən/ *noun*
Stories about characters and events that are not real.

field /fēld/ *noun*
A piece of open land, sometimes used for growing crops.

fierce /firs/ *adjective*
1. Violent or dangerous. *A lion is a fierce animal.*
2. Very strong or extreme. *The fierce wind blew down the trees.*

fierc·er /firs ər/ *adjective* More fierce.

film /film/ *noun*
1. A very thin layer of something.
2. A roll of thin plastic for photographs.

fi·nal /fī nəl/
1. *adjective* Last. **2.** *adjective* Not to be changed.
3. *noun* The last examination in a school term.

find /fīnd/
1. *verb* To discover something. **2.** *verb* To come to and state a decision. **3.** *noun* A valuable or important discovery. ▶ *verb* **finding, found**

fir /fûr/ *noun* An evergreen tree related to a pine tree. **Fir** sounds like **fur**.

flash·back /flash bak/ *noun*
1. A break in a book or movie to show something that happened earlier. **2.** A sudden memory of something.

fla·vor /flā vər/
1. *noun* Taste. **2.** *verb* To add taste to food.

fluff·y /fluf ē/ *adjective*
1. Light and airy. **2.** Covered with soft, fine hair.

fol·low /fol ō/ *verb*
1. To be guided by someone or something **2.** To go behind someone. **3.** To come after. **4.** To obey.

for·bid·den /fər bid ən/ *verb*
To have ordered someone not to do something.
▶ **forbid, forbidding, forbade**

fore·word /fôr wərd/ *noun*
A short introduction to a book. **Foreword** sounds like **forward**.

for·gave /fər gāv/ *verb*
Pardoned or excused someone. Past tense of **forgive**.

for·get / fər get/ *verb*
To not remember something. ▶ **forgetting, forgot, forgotten**

for·give /fər giv/ *verb*
To pardon someone, or to stop blaming a person for something. ▶ forgiving, forgave, forgiven

for·giv·en /fər giv ən/ *verb* Pardoned.

for·got /fər got/ *verb*
Did not remember. Past tense of **forget**.

for·got·ten /fər got ən/ *verb*
Not remembered.

for·ward /fôr wərd/
1. *adverb* Toward the front. 2. *adjective* Toward the future. **Forward** sounds like **foreword**.

fos·sil /fos əl/ *noun*
The ancient remains of an animal or a plant preserved as rock.

fought /fôt/ *verb*
Struggled with. Past tense of **fight**.

found /found/ *verb*
1. Discovered something. Past tense of **find**.
2. To set up or start something, such as a school.

foun·tain /foun tən/ *noun*
A stream of water used for drinking or decoration.

frac·ture /frak chər/
1. *verb* To break or crack something, especially a bone. 2. *noun* A break or crack.

freck·les /frek əlz/ *noun*
Small brown spots on the skin.

freeze /frēz/ *verb*
1. To make or become solid or icy at a very low temperature. 2. To stop still because of feeling frightened. ▶ freezing, froze, frozen

freight /frāt/ *noun*
Goods or cargo carried by trains, ships, planes, trucks, and so on.

fried /frīd/ *verb*
Cooked in hot oil. Past tense of **fry**.

frown /froun/ *verb*
To move your eyebrows together and wrinkle your forehead.

froze /frōz/ *verb*
Became ice. Past tense of **freeze**.

fry·ing /frī ing/ *verb*
Cooking food in hot fat or oil.

fun·ni·er /fu nē ər/ *adjective*
More amusing.

fun·ni·est /fu nē ist/ *adjective*
Most amusing.

fur /fûr/ *noun*
The thick, hairy coat of an animal. **Fur** sounds like **fir**.

fur·ni·ture /fûr nə chər/ *noun*
Things such as chairs and tables in a home or an office.

a	add	ô	order	th	this
ā	ace	o͝o	took	zh	vision
â	care	o͞o	pool		
ä	palm	u	up		
e	end	û	burn		
ē	equal	yo͞o	fuse	ə	=
i	it	oi	oil	a	in *above*
ī	ice	ou	pout	e	in *sicken*
o	odd	ng	ring	i	in *possible*
ō	open	th	thin	o	in *melon*
				u	in *circus*

fu·ture /fyoo chər/ *noun*
1. The time to come. **2.** The future tense in grammar.

fuz·zy /fuz ē/ *adjective*
1. Like or covered with fuzz. **2.** Not clear.

gent·ly /jent lē/ *adverb*
1. In a kind and sensitive way; softly. **2.** Gradually.

ges·ture /jes chər/ *verb*
To move your head or hands in order to express a feeling or idea.

gig·gled /gig əld/ *verb*
Laughed in a light-hearted way. Past tense of **giggle**.

gig·gling /gig ling/ *verb*
Laughing in a light-hearted way.

glad·ly /glad lē/ *adverb* Happily.

gloom·y /gloo mē/ *adjective*
1. Dull and dark. **2.** Sad and depressed.

gos·sip /gos ip/
1. *noun* A person who talks about other people.
2. *noun* Idle talk. **3.** *verb* To talk about others.

grief /grēf/ *noun* Extreme sadness.

groan /grōn/ *verb*
To make a long, low sound when in pain or unhappy. **Groan** sounds like **grown**.

grown /grōn/ *verb*
To have increased in size. **Grown** sounds like **groan**.

grum·ble /grum bəl/ *verb*
To complain about something in a grouchy way.

hair /hâr/ *noun*
The fine strands that grow on a person or animal. **Hair** sounds like **hare**.

half /haf/
1. *noun* One of two equal parts. **2.** *adverb* Partly or not completely.

halves /havz/ *noun*
Two equal parts.

ham·burg·er /ham bûr gər/ *noun*
1. Ground beef sandwich in a bun. **2.** Ground beef.

Word History

The **hamburger**, a favorite American sandwich, is actually named after the German city of Hamburg, where the ground beef steak originated.

hap·pen /hap ən/ *verb* To take place; occur.

hap·pi·ly /hap ə lē/ *adverb*
1. In a pleased, contented manner. **2.** Luckily.

har·bor /här bər/
1. *noun* A place where ships shelter or unload.
2. *verb* To take care of or hide someone or something.

hard·ware /härd wâr/ *noun*
1. Tools and other household equipment.
2. Computer equipment, such as a printer or monitor.

hare /hâr/ *noun*
An animal like a large rabbit with long, strong back legs. **Hare** sounds like **hair**.

harm·ful /härm fəl/ *adjective*
Causing injury or hurt.

harm·less /härm lis/ *adjective*
Not able to cause injury or damage.

head·ache /hed āk/ *noun*
A pain in the head.

head·quar·ters /hed kwôr tərz/ *noun*
The place from which an organization is run.

health /helth/ *noun*
1. Strength and fitness. 2. The condition of your body.

heaped /hēpt/ *verb*
Piled on. Past tense of **heap**.

heap·ing /hēp ing/ *verb* Piling on.

height /hīt/ *noun*
A measurement of how tall someone or something is.

help·ful /help fəl/ *adjective*
Friendly and willing to help.

help·less /help lis/ *adjective*
Unable to look after one's self.

high·er /hīr/ *adjective*
A greater distance from the ground. **Higher** sounds like **hire**.

hire /hīr/ *verb*
To employ someone. **Hire** sounds like **higher**.

hoarse /hôrs/ *adjective* Sounding rough and sore.
Hoarse sounds like **horse**.

hope·ful /hōp fəl/ *adjective* Feeling hope.

hope·ful·ly /hōp fəl le/ *adverb*
In a hopeful manner.

hope·less /hōp lis/ *adjective*
1. Without hope. 2. Bad, or lacking in skill.

hope·less·ly /hōp lis lē/ *adverb*
In a hopeless manner.

hor·ror /hôr ər/ *noun*
1. Great fear; terror. 2. Something that causes terror.

horse /hôrs/ *noun*
A large, strong animal with hoofs that people ride.
Horse sounds like **hoarse**.

ho·tel /ho tel/ *noun*
A place where one pays to stay overnight.

howl /houl/ *verb*
1. To make loud, drawn-out cries. 2. To yell out with laughter.

hugged /hugd/ *verb* Held someone or something tightly in a loving way. Past tense of **hug**.

hug·ging /hug ing/ *verb* Holding someone or something tightly in a loving way.

hun·gry /hung grē/ *adjective* Wanting food.

a	add	ô	order	ŧh	this
ā	ace	o͞o	took	zh	vision
â	care	o͞o	pool		
ä	palm	u	up		
e	end	û	burn	ə	=
ē	equal	yo͞o	fuse	a	in *above*
i	it	oi	oil	e	in *sicken*
ī	ice	ou	pout	i	in *possible*
o	odd	ng	ring	o	in *melon*
ō	open	th	thin	u	in *circus*

I i

in·jure /in jər/ *verb*
To hurt or harm yourself or someone else.

in·stead /in sted/ *adverb* In place of another.

J j

jam·bo·ree /jam bə rē/ *noun* A loud, lively party.

K k

knee /nē/ *noun*
The joint between the upper and lower leg that bends when walking.

knew /nōō or nyōō/ *verb*
Was familiar with a person, place, or piece of information. Past tense of **know**.

knife /nīf/ *noun*
A tool with a sharp blade. *plural* **knives**

knight /nīt/ *noun*
1. In medieval times, a warrior who fought on horseback. **2.** In Great Britain, a man who has been given the title "Sir."

knives /nīvz/ *noun*
Tools with sharp blades. Plural of **knife**.

knock /nok/
1. *verb* To bang or hit something. **2.** *noun* A sharp blow or rap, or the sound accompanying it.

knot /not/
1. *noun* A fastening made by looping and twisting one or more pieces of string or rope. **2.** *verb* To make a knot. ▶ *verb* **knotting, knotted**

know /nō/ *verb*
To be familiar with a person, place, or piece of information. ▶ **knowing, knew, known**

know·ledge /nol ij/ *noun*
The things or ideas that someone knows; information.

known /nōn/ *verb* To have been aware.

knuck·les /nuk əlz/ *noun* Finger joints.

L l

lamb /lam/ *noun*
1. A young sheep. **2.** Meat from a young sheep.

la·ser /lā zər/ *noun*
A device that makes a beam of light that can be used for light shows, for cutting things, or for operations.

late·ly /lāt lē/ *adverb* Recently.

la·zy /lā zē/ *adjective* Not wanting to work.

lead /lēd/ **1.** *verb* To show someone the way. **2.** To be in charge. **3.** /led/ *noun* A soft, grey metal.
▶ *verb* **leading, led**

leaf /lēf/
1. *noun* A flat green part of a plant or tree that grows out from a stem, twig, or branch. **2.** *noun* Page in a book. **3.** **Idiom: Turn over a new leaf** means start over; try to do better in the future. *plural* **leaves**

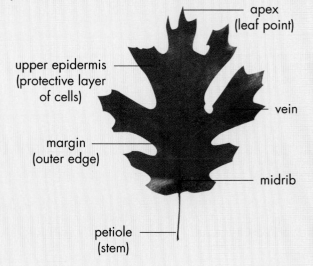

apex (leaf point)

upper epidermis (protective layer of cells)

vein

margin (outer edge)

midrib

petiole (stem)

least /lēst/
1. *noun* The smallest amount. **2.** *adverb* Less than anything else.

leave /lēv/ *verb*
1. To go away. **2.** To let something stay or remain.

leaves /lēvz/ *noun*
Parts of a plant or tree. Plural of **leaf**.

left /left/ *verb* Went away. Past tense of **leave**.

left·o·ver /left ō vər/ *noun*
The part of a meal that has not been eaten.

lem·on /lem ən/ *noun* A yellow citrus fruit.

les·son /les ən/ *noun*
1. Some information or skill that you need to learn or study. **2.** A set period of time in school when pupils are taught. **3.** An experience that teaches.

let·ter /let ər/ *noun*
1. A part of the alphabet that stands for a sound.
2. A written message to or from someone.

life /līf/ *noun*
1. The quality that separates people, animals, and plants from things that are not alive, such as rocks.
2. The time of being alive. *plural* **lives**

life·time /līf tīm/ *noun*
The period of time of being alive.

light·en /līt ən/ *verb*
1. To make brighter or lighter. **2.** To make or become lighter in color. **3.** To make or become lighter in weight.

limb /lim/ *noun*
1. A part of a body used in moving, such as arms, legs, wings, or flippers. **2.** A branch of a tree.

lim·ber /lim bər/
1. *adjective* Bending or moving easily. **2.** *verb* To stretch your muscles before exercising.

li·on /lī ən/ *noun*
A large, light brown wildcat found in Africa and southern Asia.

lit·er·a·ture /lit er ə chər/ *noun*
Written works, including novels, plays, short stories, essays, and poems.

lit·tle /lit əl/
1. *adjective* Small in size or amount.
2. *noun* A small amount of something.

lives /līvz/ *noun*
Lifetimes. The plural of **life**.

li·zard /liz ərd/ *noun*
A reptile with a scaly body, four legs, and a long tail.

loaf /lōf/ *noun*
1. Bread baked in one piece. **2.** Food the shape of baked bread. *plural* **loaves**

loaves /lōvz/ *noun*
Foods shaped like bread. The plural of **loaf**.

lone·ly /lōn lē/ *adjective*
1. Feeling alone. **2.** Far from other people or things.

loos·en /lōō sən/ *verb*
To make something less tight.

a	add	ô	order	ŧh	this
ā	ace	o͝o	took	zh	vision
â	care	o͞o	pool		
ä	palm	u	up		
e	end	û	burn	ə	=
ē	equal	yo͞o	fuse	a	in *above*
i	it	oi	oil	e	in *sicken*
ī	ice	ou	pout	i	in *possible*
o	odd	ng	ring	o	in *melon*
ō	open	th	thin	u	in *circus*

love·li·est /luv lē ist/ *adjective* Most lovely.

luck·i·ly /luk ə lē/ *adverb* Fortunately.

lum·ber /lum bər/ *noun*
Wood or timber that has been sawed.

lump·y /lum pē/ *adjective* Full of lumps.

M m

man·sion /man shən/ *noun* A very large house.

mar·ried /ma rēd/ *verb*
Went through a ceremony to become husband and wife. Past tense of **marry**.

mar·ry·ing /ma rē ing/ *verb*
Going through a ceremony to become husband and wife.

meal /mēl/ *noun*
Food that is served and eaten, usually at a particular time of day.

mean /mēn/ *verb*
1. To say or express something. **2.** Intend to do something. *I mean to go skating tomorrow.*
▶ **meaning, meant**

meant /ment/ *verb*
1. Said or expressed something. **2.** Intended to do something. Past tense of **mean**.

mea·sles /mē zəlz/ *noun, plural*
A disease causing fever and a rash.

meas·ure /mezh ər/ *verb*
1. To find out the size, weight, and capacity of something.

mem·ber /mem bər/ *noun*
1. A person, animal, or thing that belongs to a group.
2. A part of the body, such as an arm or a leg.

men·tion /men shən/ *verb*
To speak or write about something briefly.

mer·ry-go-round /mer ē gō round/ *noun*
A circular platform driven round by machinery, with a set of animal figures and seats on it that children ride for fun.

mid·dle /mid əl/ *adjective*
Half way between two things, sides, or outer points.

mil·lion /mil yən/ *noun*
A thousand thousands (1,000,000).

mir·ror /mir ər/ *noun*
A metal or glass surface that reflects an image.

mix·ture /miks chər/ *noun*
A combination of different things.

mois·ture /mois chər/ *noun*
1. Water or other liquid in the air or on a surface.
2. Slight wetness.

mo·ment /mō mənt/ *noun*
A very brief period of time.

most·ly /mōst lē/ *adverb* Mainly or usually.

moun·tain /moun tən/ *noun*
1. A very high piece of land. **2.** A large amount of something.

mud·dy /mud ē/
1. *adjective* Covered with wet, sticky earth.
2. *verb* To make something unclear.

muf·fin /muf ən/ *noun*
A small cake or bread shaped like a cupcake.

mul·ti·ply·ing /mul tə plī ing/ *verb*
1. Adding the same number to itself several times, as in *multiplying 3 times 4 to get 12.* **2.** Growing in number. *The weeds keep multiplying.*

mum·ble /mum bəl/ *verb*
To speak quietly and unclearly with the lips nearly closed. ▶ mumbling, mumbled

N n

na·tion /nā shən/ *noun*
A large group of people who live in the same part of the world and often share the same government.

na·ture /nā chər/ *noun*
1. Everything in the world that is not made by people, such as plants, animals, and mountains. **2.** The character of someone or something. *She has a very sweet nature.*

need·ed /nēd əd/ *verb*
Wanted something. Past tense of **need**.

need·ing /nēd ing/ *verb* Wanting something.

need·less /nēd lis/ *adjective* Not necessary.

need·less·ly /nēd lis lē/ *adverb*
In a wasteful or unnecessary manner.

neigh·bor /nā bər/ *noun*
1. A person who lives next door to you or near to you. **2.** A person, place, or thing that is next to or near another.

nei·ther /nē ther or nī ther/
1. *adjective* Not either. **2.** *pronoun* Not either one.
3. *conjunction* Used with **nor** to show two negative choices. *Neither Kim nor Paul came to the party.*

neph·ew /nef yoo/ *noun*
The son of someone's brother or sister.

nev·er·the·less /nev ər thə les/ *adverb*
In spite of that; yet.

nic·kel /nik əl/ *noun*
1. A United States coin equal to five cents. **2.** A hard, silver-gray metal.

niece /nēs/ *noun*
The daughter of someone's brother or sister.

nod·ded /nod əd/ *verb*
Moved your head up and down, especially to say *yes.* Past tense of **nod**.

nod·ding /nod ing/ *verb*
Moving your head up and down, especially to say *yes.*

nois·y /noi zē/ *adjective* Loud.

non·sense /non sens/ *noun*
Talk, writing, or behavior that is silly or has no meaning.

non·stop /non stop/ *adjective*
Without any stops or breaks, as in *a nonstop flight.*

noo·dle /noo dəl/ *noun*
A flat or round strand of dough.

a	add	ô	order	th	this
ā	ace	oo	took	zh	vision
â	care	oo	pool		
ä	palm	u	up		
e	end	û	burn	ə	=
ē	equal	yoo	fuse	a	in *above*
i	it	oi	oil	e	in *sicken*
ī	ice	ou	pout	i	in *possible*
o	odd	ng	ring	o	in *melon*
ō	open	th	thin	u	in *circus*

note·book /nōt boŏk/ *noun*
A small pad or book of paper used for writing notes.

no·tice /nō tis/
1. *verb* To see something, or to become aware of it.
2. *noun* A written message displayed in a public place.
▶ *verb* noticing, noticed

no·ticed /nō tist/ *verb*
Saw something or became aware of it. Past tense of **notice**.

no·tic·ing /nō tis ing/ *verb*
Seeing something or becoming aware of it.

numb /num/ *adjective*
Unable to feel anything, or unable to move.

num·ber /num bər/ *noun*
1. A word or symbol that tells how many. 2. A word that identifies someone or something, such as *a telephone number*.

 O o

o·cean /ō shən/ *noun*
The body of salt water that covers about 71 percent of the earth's surface.

off /ôf/
1. *preposition* Away from. 2. *adverb* Away from a place. 3. *adverb* Not turned on or not working.

of·fer /ôf ər/ *verb*
1. To ask if someone would like something.
2. To say that you are willing to do something.

of·fice /ôf is/ *noun*
A part of a building in which people work, usually at desks.

of·ten /ôf ən/ *adverb* Many times.

on·ion /un yən/ *noun*
A round vegetable with a strong smell and taste.

Word History

Onion comes from the Latin word *unio*, which means "oneness" or "union." If you cut an onion in half, you'll find out why this vegetable is a "union" of many different layers. The onion has been a symbol of strength. Civil War general Ulysses S. Grant once refused to move his troops until he received a shipment of onions to keep his soldiers strong.

on·ly /ōn lē/
1. *adverb* Not more than; just. 2. *adjective* With nothing or no one else. 3. *conjunction* But.

o·pen /ō pən/
1. *adjective* Not shut or closed. 2. *adjective* Not covered or enclosed. 3. *verb* To start or begin something.

o·pin·ion /ə pin yən/ *noun*
1. The ideas and beliefs that you have about something. 2. An expert's judgment.

or·di·nar·i·ly /ôr də nâr ə lē/ *adverb*
Usually; regularly.

or·gan /ôr gən/ *noun*
1. A large musical instrument with one or more keyboards and many pipes. 2. A part of the body that does a certain job. *The lungs are the organs for breathing.*

or·phan /ôr fən/ *noun*
A child whose parents are dead.

ought /ôt/ *verb*
1. To show an obligation or a duty. *You ought to keep your promises.* 2. To show what is expected or likely.

o·ver /ō vər/
1. *preposition* Above or on top of something.
2. *preposition* More than.
3. *adjective* Finished.
4. *preposition* Across.
5. *adverb* Remaining or extra.

owl /oul/ *noun*
A bird that has a round head, large eyes, and a hooked bill.

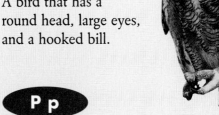

P p

pain /pān/ *noun*
A feeling of hurt or great unhappiness. **Pain** sounds like **pane**.

pane /pān/ *noun*
A sheet of glass or plastic in a window or door. **Pane** sounds like **pain**.

pa·per /pā pər/ *noun*
1. A thin sheet of material made from wood pulp and rags, used for writing, printing, and drawing. 2. A written report for school. 3. A newspaper.

pa·per·back /pā pər bak/ *noun*
A book with a paper cover.

part·ly /pärt lē/ *adverb*
In part. *He was partly to blame for breaking the lamp.*

pas·ture /pas chər/ *noun*
Grazing land for animals.

pat·tern /pat ərn/ *noun*
1. A repeating order of colors, shapes, and figures.
2. A sample or model that you can copy from.

pause /pôz/ *verb*
To stop for a short time. **Pause** sounds like **paws**.

paws /pôz/ *noun*
The feet of an animal having four feet and claws. **Paws** sounds like **pause**.

peace /pēs/ *noun*
1. A period without war or fighting. 2. Calmness of mind or place. **Peace** sounds like **piece**.

peace·ful /pēs fəl/ *adjective*
1. Full of peace; calm. 2. Liking peace.

peace·ful·ly /pēs fəl lē/ *adverb*
In a peaceful manner.

peo·ple /pē pəl/ *noun*
1. Persons or human beings. 2. A collection of human beings who make up a nation, race, tribe, or group.
3. Family or relatives.

pep·per /pep ər/ *noun*
1. A spicy powder. 2. A hollow vegetable that is usually red, green, or yellow.

per·son /pûr sən/ *noun*
1. An individual human being. 2. In grammar, the first person refers to "I" or "we," the second person refers to "you," the third person refers to "he," "she," "it," or "they."

pho·to·graph /fō tə graf/ *noun*
A picture taken by a camera.

a	add	ô	order	th	this	
ā	ace	o͝o	took	zh	vision	
â	care	o͞o	pool			
ä	palm	u	up	ə	=	
e	end	û	burn		a	in *above*
ē	equal	yo͞o	fuse		e	in *sicken*
i	it	oi	oil		i	in *possible*
ī	ice	ou	pout		o	in *melon*
o	odd	ng	ring		u	in *circus*
ō	open	th	thin			

phys·i·cal /fiz ə kəl/ *adjective*
1. Having to do with the body as in *physical fitness*.
2. Having to do with matter and energy as in *physical science*.

pic·ture /pik chər/
1. *noun* An image of something, such as a painting, photograph, or drawing. **2.** *noun* An image on a television screen. **3.** *noun* A movie. **4.** *verb* To imagine something.

piece /pēs/ *noun*
1. A bit or section of something larger. **2.** Something written or made. **Piece** sounds like **peace**.

pi·geon /pij ən/ *noun*
A plump bird often found in cities.

pil·low /pil ō/ *noun*
A large, soft cushion, especially one on which you put your head when you are sleeping.

pi·lot /pī lət/
1. *noun* Someone who flies an aircraft. **2.** *noun* Someone who steers a ship in and out of port.
3. *verb* To control or guide something.

pi·rate /pī rət/ *noun*
Someone who robbed ships at sea long ago.

play·ful /plā fəl/ *adjective*
1. Willing to play. **2.** Humorous, or meant to amuse.

play·ful·ly /plā fə lē/ *adverb*
In a playful manner.

pleas·ant /plez ənt/ *adjective*
1. Enjoyable or giving pleasure. **2.** Likable or friendly.

please /plēz/
1. *verb* To satisfy or to give pleasure. **2.** *adverb* A polite word used when you ask for something. **3.** *verb* To choose or to prefer. ▶ *verb* **pleasing, pleased**

pleased /plēzd/ *verb* Satisfied. Past tense of **please**.

pleas·ing /plēz ing/ *verb* Giving pleasure.

plea·sure /plezh ər/ *noun*
A feeling of enjoyment or satisfaction.

poo·dle /poo dəl/ *noun*
A breed of dog with tight, curly fur that is usually cut in a fancy style.

Word History

While we think of **poodle** as French, the breed's name actually comes from the German word, *Pudelhund*, which means "dog that splashes in the water." These intelligent dogs are skilled at swimming and retrieving sticks from ponds and lakes.

po·si·tion /pə zish ən/
1. *noun* The place where someone or something is.
2. *verb* To put something in a certain place.
3. *noun* A person's opinion on a certain issue.

pounce /pouns/ *verb*
To jump on something suddenly and grab hold of it. ▶ **pouncing, pounced**

pound /pound/
1. *noun* A unit of weight equal to 16 ounces.
2. *noun* A unit of money used in England, Ireland, and elsewhere. **3.** *verb* To keep hitting something with force, as in *pound the nail*. **4.** *noun* A place where stray animals are kept.

pow·der /pou dər/
1. *noun* Tiny particles made by grinding, crushing, or pounding a solid substance. **2.** *noun* A form of makeup or other product made from powder. **3.** *verb* To make or turn something into powder.

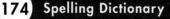

pow·er /pou ər/ *noun*
1. The strength or ability to do something.
2. The right to command, control, or make decisions.
3. A person, group, or nation that has great strength or influence. **4.** Electricity or other forms of energy.

pres·sure /presh ər/ *noun*
1. The force produced by pressing on something.
2. Strong influence, force, or persuasion.

price·less /prīs lis/ *adjective*
Too precious for anyone to put a value on.

prize /prīz/
1. *noun* A reward for winning a game or contest. **2.** *verb* To value something very much.
▶ *verb* prizing, prized

pro·fes·sor /prə fes ər/ *noun*
A teacher at a college or university.

prom·ised /prom isd/ *verb*
Made a vow. Past tense of **promise.**

prom·is·ing /prom is ing/ *verb*
Making a vow.

pud·dle /pud əl/ *noun*
A small pool of liquid.

pum·per·nick·el /pum pər nik əl/ *noun*
A heavy, dark bread made from rye.

pup·pet /pup it/ *noun*
A toy in the shape of a person or an animal that a person can control with strings or a hand.

push·o·ver /pŏŏsh ō vər/ *noun*
1. Something extremely easy to do.
2. A person who is easy to take advantage of.

puz·zle /puz əl/
1. *noun* A toy or a game that tests one's mental skills, such as a picture puzzle. **2.** *noun* Someone or something that is hard to understand. **3.** *verb* To become confused. ▶ *verb* puzzling, puzzled

Q q

quack /kwak/ *verb*
A sharp, loud sound made by a duck.

quar·ter /kwôr tər/ *noun*
1. One of four equal parts. **2.** A coin of the United States and Canada equal to 25 cents.

queen /kwēn/ *noun*
1. A woman who is the ruler of a country. **2.** The wife of a king.

ques·tion /kwes chən/
1. *noun* A sentence that asks something. **2.** *noun* A problem, or something that needs to be asked about.
3. *verb* To ask.

quick /kwik/ *adjective* Fast.

quick·ly /kwik lē/ *adverb* In a fast manner.

qui·et /kwī ət/
1. *adjective* Not loud. *I spoke in a quiet voice.*
2. *adjective* Peaceful and calm. *We spent a quiet afternoon.* **3.** *noun* The state of being quiet. *The teacher asked for quiet.*

a	add	ô	order	th	this
ā	ace	ŏŏ	took	zh	vision
â	care	ōō	pool		
ä	palm	u	up		
e	end	û	burn		
ē	equal	yōō	fuse	ə	=
i	it	oi	oil	a	in *above*
ī	ice	ou	pout	e	in *sicken*
o	odd	ng	ring	i	in *possible*
ō	open	th	thin	o	in *melon*
				u	in *circus*

qui·et·ly /kwī ət lē/ *adverb* In a quiet way.

quilt /kwilt/ *noun*
A warm covering for a bed, like a blanket.

quirk·y /kwûrk ē/ *adjective*
Peculiar, strange.

quit /kwit/ *verb*
1. To stop doing something. 2. To leave something.
▶ quitting, quit or quitted

quite /kwīt/ *adverb*
1. Completely. 2. Actually or really. 3. Very.

ra·di·o /rā dē ō/
1. *noun* A device that sends or receives broadcasts and changes them into sound. 2. *verb* To send a message using a radio.

rain·y /rā nē/ *adjective* Having rain.

read·y /red ē/ *adjective*
1. Prepared. 2. Willing. 3. About to do something.

re·al·ly /rē ə lē or rē lē/ *adverb*
1. Actually. 2. Very.

rea·son /rē zən/
1. *noun* The cause of something or the motive behind it. *There was no reason to hurry.* 2. *noun* An explanation. 3. *verb* To think in a logical way. *I reasoned that it would be quicker to walk.*

re·ceive /ri sēv/ *verb*
1. To accept something. 2. To experience. 3. To welcome.

re·la·tion /ri lā shən/ *noun*
A member of your family.

re·lief /ri lēf/ *noun*
1. A feeling of freedom from pain or worry. 2. Aid given to people in special need.

re·mem·ber /ri mem bər/ *verb*
1. To recall or to bring back to mind. 2. To keep in mind carefully.

re·peat /ri pēt/ *verb*
To say or do something again.

re·plied /ri plīd/ *verb*
Responded. Past tense of **reply.** ▶ reply, replies

re·ply·ing /ri plī ing/ *verb*
Responding.

rest·less /rest ləs/ *adjective*
Not able to keep still or to concentrate on anything.

re·view /ri vyōō/
1. *noun* A written opinion about a new book, play, movie, or such. 2. *verb* To study something carefully. 3. *verb* To study or go over again. 4. *verb* To make a formal inspection of.

rhym·ing /rīm ing/ *verb*
Ending with the same sounds.

rib·bon /rib ən/ *noun*
A long, thin band used for tying hair or decorating a present.

ro·bin /rob in/ *noun*
A songbird that has a reddish orange chest.

root /rōōt or rŏŏt/
1. *noun* The part of a plant or tree that grows underground. 2. *verb* To form roots. **Root** sounds like **route.**

rough /ruf/ *adjective*
1. Not smooth but with dents or bumps. 2. Not gentle.

round /round/
1. *adjective* Shaped like a circle or a ball.
2. *adjective* Having a curved surface or outline.
3. *preposition* Around.

route /rō͞ot or rout/ *noun*
The road you follow to get from one place to another. **Route** sounds like **root**.

run·way /run wā/ *noun*
A road for the takeoff and landing of aircraft.

sad·der /sad ər/ *adjective* More unhappy.

sad·dest /sad ist/ *adjective* Most unhappy.

sad·ly /sad lē/ *adjective* In a sad way.

sam·ple /sam pəl/
1. *noun* A small amount of something that shows what the whole is like. 2. *verb* To try a small amount to see if you like it. ▶ *verb* **sampling, sampled**

san·dy /san dē/ *adjective*
1. Covered with sand. 2. The color of sand.

sat·is·fied /sat is fīd/ *verb*
Met the needs or wants of; pleased. *She was satisfied with her grade.* ▶ **satisfy, satisfies, satisfying**

scarf /skärf/ *noun*
A strip of material worn around the neck or head.

scarves /skärvz/ *noun* Plural of **scarf**.

scat·ter /skat ər/ *verb*
1. To throw things over a wide area. 2. To hurry away in different directions. ▶ **scattering, scattered**

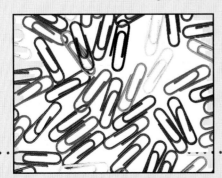

scram·ble /skram bəl/ *verb*
1. To climb over rocks or hills. 2. To rush or struggle to get somewhere or something. 3. To mix up or mix together. ▶ **scrambling, scrambled**

seek /sēk/ *verb*
1. To look or search for something. 2. To try. 3. To ask for. ▶ **seeking, sought**

sel·ler /sel ər/ *noun*
A person who sells something. **Seller** sounds like **cellar**.

shelf /shelf/ *noun*
A horizontal board on a wall, in a cabinet, or in a bookcase used for holding or storing things.

shelves /shelvz/ *noun*
Horizontal boards used for holding or storing things. Plural of **shelf**.

shield /shēld/
1. *noun* A piece of armor carried to protect the body from attack. 2. *verb* To protect something or someone.

shin·y /shī nē/ *adjective*
Shining; bright.

shone /shōn/ *verb*
1. Gave off light. 2. Brightened by polishing. Past tense of **shine**. **Shone** sounds like **shown**.

a	add	ô	order	th	this
ā	ace	ō͞o	took	zh	vision
â	care	ō͞o	pool		
ä	palm	u	up		
e	end	û	burn		
ē	equal	yō͞o	fuse	ə	=
i	it	oi	oil	a	in *above*
ī	ice	ou	pout	e	in *sicken*
o	odd	ng	ring	i	in *possible*
ō	open	th	thin	o	in *melon*
				u	in *circus*

shopped /shopt/ *verb*
Bought in a store. Past tense of **shop**.

shop·ping /shop ing/
1. *verb* Buying in stores. 2. *noun* The act of buying in stores.

shout·ed /shout ed/ *verb*
Yelled. Past tense of **shout**.

shout·ing /shout ing/ *verb* Yelling.

show·er /shou ər/
1. *noun* A piece of equipment that produces a fine spray of water for washing the body. 2. *verb* To wash yourself under a shower. 3. *noun* A short rainfall.

shown /shōn/ *verb*
1. Allowed to see or be seen. 2. Appeared. Past tense of **show**. **Shown** sounds like **shone**.

shuf·fled /shuf əld/ *verb*
1. Walked slowly and dragged the feet. 2. Mixed the order of playing cards. Past tense of **shuffle**.

si·lent /sī lənt/ *adjective* Absolutely quiet.

sil·li·er /sil ē ər/ *adjective* Funnier.

sil·li·est /sil ē ist/ *adjective* Funniest.

sil·ver /sil vər/ *noun*
1. A shiny, whitish metal used to make jewelry, coins, and other objects. 2. The color of silver.

sim·i·lar /sim ə lər/ *adjective*
Alike, or of the same type.

sim·ple /sim pəl/ *adjective*
1. Easy, or not hard to understand or do.
2. With nothing added. 3. Plain; not fancy.

sim·pler /sim plər/ *adjective*
1. Easier. 2. Plainer; less fancy.

sim·plest /sim plist/ *adjective*
1. Easiest. 2. Plainest; least fancy.

sim·ply /sim plē/ *adverb*
1. In a simple way; easily. 2. Merely; just. 3. Very.

size /sīz/ *noun*
1. The measurement of how large or small something is. 2. One in a series of standard clothing measurements.

skate·board /skāt bôrd/ *noun*
A small board with wheels that one stands on and rides.

skill·ful /skil fəl/ *adjective* Can do something well.

sleep /slēp/ *verb* To rest in an unaware state; the opposite of to wake up. ▶ **sleeping, slept**

sleep·y /slē pē/ *adjective* Drowsy; ready for sleep.

sleigh /slā/ *noun*
A large sled pulled over snow or ice, usually by horses. **Sleigh** sounds like **slay**.

slept /slept/ *verb* Rested in an unaware state. Past tense of **sleep**.

slip·per·y /slip ə rē/ *adjective* Smooth, wet, oily; hard to walk on or to hold on to.

slow·ly /slō lē/ *adverb* In a slow way.

sneeze /snēz/ *verb*
To push out air suddenly through your nose and mouth. ▶ **sneezing, sneezed**

Word History

Sneeze was originally spelled with an *f: fnese*. In Old English, *s* was written like this: *ſ*, and it looked a lot like an *f*. The two letters got confused, and in time *fnese* became *sneeze*.

sol·dier /sol jər/ *noun* A person who is in the army.

sought /sôt/ *verb*
1. Looked for or searched for something. 2. Asked for. Past tense of **seek**.

sound /sound/
1. *noun* Something that is heard. 2. *verb* To make a noise. 3. *adjective* Healthy, as in *a sound mind*.

spar·kle /spär kəl/ *verb*
To shine with many flashing points of light.

speak /spēk/
1. *verb* To talk or say words out loud. 2. *verb* To tell or make known your ideas, opinions or feelings. 3. **Idiom:** If you **speak out** or **speak up**, you speak loudly or you speak openly and honestly about what you really believe.

spi·der /spī dər/ *noun*
A small animal with eight legs and a body with two parts. Spiders spin webs to trap insects for food.

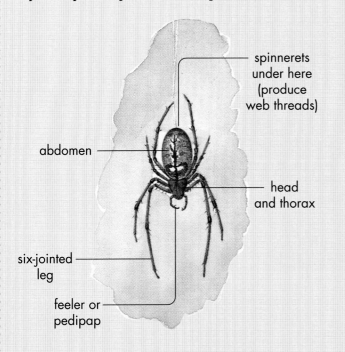

spinnerets under here (produce web threads)

abdomen

head and thorax

six-jointed leg

feeler or pedipap

spied /spīd/ *verb* 1. Watched closely or secretly. 2. Saw. Past tense of **spy**.

spi·ral /spī rəl/ *adjective*
Winding around in circles like a spring.

splash·down /splash doun/ *noun*
The landing of a spacecraft in the ocean.

spoke /spōk/
1. *verb* Talked. 2. *verb* Made a speech. 3. *verb* Used or was able to use (a language) in speech, as in *spoke Spanish*. Past tense of **speak**. 4. *noun* One of the thin rods that connect the rim of a wheel to the hub.

spo·ken /spō kən/ *verb* Have talked.

spread /spred/ *verb*
1. To unfold or to stretch out. 2. To cover a surface with something. 3. To reach out or extend over.

spy·ing /spī ing/ *verb*
Watching someone secretly.

square /skwâr/ *noun*
1. A shape with four equal sides and four right angles. 2. An open area with streets on four sides.

squeak /skwēk/ *verb*
To make a short, high sound like a mouse.

squeeze /skwēz/ *verb*
1. To press something firmly from opposite sides. 2. To force something into or through a space.

squig·gle /skwig əl/
1. *noun* A wiggly twist. 2. *verb* To make with twisting lines. ▶ *verb* squiggling, squiggled

squir·rel /skwûr əl/ *noun*
A small animal that climbs trees and has a bushy tail.

a	add	ô	order	th	this
ā	ace	o͝o	took	zh	vision
â	care	o͞o	pool		
ä	palm	u	up		
e	end	û	burn	ə	=
ē	equal	yo͞o	fuse	a	in *above*
i	it	oi	oil	e	in *sicken*
ī	ice	ou	pout	i	in *possible*
o	odd	ng	ring	o	in *melon*
ō	open	th	thin	u	in *circus*

stal·lion /stal yən/ *noun* An adult male horse.

stared /stârd/ *verb* Looked at someone or something for a long time. Past tense of **stare**.
▶ stare, staring

star·ing /stâr ing/ *verb*
Looking at someone or something for a long time.

sta·tion /stā shən/ *noun*
1. A place for passengers where tickets for trains or buses are sold. **2.** A building where a service is provided, as in *a fire station*. **3.** A place that sends out television or radio signals.

stead·y /sted ē/
1. *adjective* Continuous and not changing much.
2. *adjective* Firm or stable. **3.** *verb* To stop something from moving about or shaking. **4.** *adjective* Sensible and dependable.

steal /stēl/ *verb*
To take something that does not belong to you.
Steal sounds like **steel**.

steel /stēl/ *noun*
A hard, strong metal made mostly from iron.
Steel sounds like **steal**.

stir·rup /stûr əp/ *noun*
The ring below a saddle that holds a horseback rider's foot.

strange·ly /strānj lē/ *adverb*
In an unusual or odd way.

strang·er /strān jər/
1. *noun* Someone you do not know. **2.** *noun* Someone who is in a place where he or she has not been before. **3.** *adjective* Odder or more unusual.

strang·est /strān jist/ *adjective*
Oddest or most unusual.

struc·ture /struk chər/ *noun*
1. Something that has been built. **2.** The organization of something or the way it is organized.

stum·ble /stum bəl/ *verb*
1. To trip; to walk in an unsteady way. **2.** To make mistakes when you are talking.

sud·den /sud ən/ *adjective*
1. Happening without warning. **2.** Quick; hasty.

suf·fer /suf ər/ *verb*
1. To have pain, discomfort, or sorrow.
2. To experience something unpleasant.

sum·mer /sum ər/ *noun*
The season between spring and autumn, when the weather is warmest.

sun·ny /sun ē/ *adjective*
Having much sunlight.

su·per /sōō pər/ *adjective* Very good; excellent.

sup·per /sup ər/ *noun* An evening meal.

sup•plied /sə plīd/ *verb*
Provided something that was needed. Past tense of **supply**. ▶ supply, supplying

sup·ply·ing /sə plī ing/ *verb*
Providing something that is needed.

sur·prise /sər prīz/ *verb*
1. To amaze or astonish someone. **2.** To come upon suddenly. ▶ surprising, surprised

sweat·shirt /swet shûrt/ *noun*
A loose-fitting, casual top with long sleeves made of heavy cloth and sometimes worn during exercise.

tail /tāl/ *noun*
1. A part that sticks out at the back end of an animal's body. **2.** Something that is shaped like a tail, as in *the tail of a kite*. **Tail** sounds like **tale**.

tale /tāl/ *noun*
1. A story. **2.** A story that is not true; a lie. **Tale** sounds like **tail**.

taught /tôt/ *verb*
Gave someone a lesson; showed someone how to do something. Past tense of **teach**.

teach /tēch/ *verb*
To give a lesson; to show someone how to do something. ▶ **teaches, teaching, taught**

tease /tēz/ *verb*
To make fun of someone. ▶ **teasing, teased**

teased /tēzd/ *verb*
Made fun of someone. Past tense of **tease**.

teas·ing /tēz ing/ *verb* Making fun of someone.

tel·e·phone /tel ə fōn/ *noun*
1. An electrical system for sending sounds over distances. 2. A device for sending and receiving these sounds. The telephone was invented by Alexander Graham Bell in 1876.

tem·per·a·ture /tem pûr ə chər/ *noun*
1. The degree of heat or cold in something, measured by a thermometer. 2. A condition when a body is hotter than normal because of illness; fever.

thank·ful /thangk fəl/ *adjective* Grateful.

thank·less /thangk lis/ *adjective*
1. Not appreciated. 2. Not likely to give thanks.

thief /thēf/ *noun* Someone who steals things.

think /thingk/ *verb*
1. To use your mind; to form an idea or to make decisions. 2. To have an opinion. 3. To have as a thought; to imagine. 4. To remember.
▶ **thinking, thought**

thirst·y /thûr stē/ *adjective*
Needing or wanting to drink something.

thor·ough /thûr ō/ *adjective*
Does a job carefully and completely.

thor·ough·fare /thûr ō fâr/ *noun* A main road.

though /thō/
1. *conjunction* In spite of the fact that; although.
2. *conjunction* Yet; but; however. 3. *adverb* However.

thought /thôt/
1. *noun* An idea or an opinion. 2. *verb* Used one's mind; had an idea. Past tense of **think**. 3. *noun* The act of thinking.

thought·ful /thôt fəl/ *adjective*
1. Serious and involving a lot of thought.
2. Considering other people's feelings.

thought·less /thôt lis/ *adjective*
1. Careless. 2. Not considering other people's feelings.

threw /thrōō/ *verb*
Sent through the air; flung; hurled. Past tense of **throw**. **Threw** sounds like **through**.

through /thrōō/ *preposition*
1. In one side and out the other. 2. To many places in; around. 3. By way of; because of. 4. As a result of. 5. From beginning to end. **Through** sounds like **threw**.

through·out /thrōō out/
1. *preposition* All the way through. 2. *adverb* In every part; everywhere.

thrown /thrōn/ *verb*
Tossed. **Thrown** sounds like **throne**.

a	add	ô	order	th	this
ā	ace	o͞o	took	zh	vision
â	care	o͞o	pool		
ä	palm	u	up		
e	end	û	burn		
ē	equal	yo͞o	fuse	ə	=
i	it	oi	oil	a	in *above*
ī	ice	ou	pout	e	in *sicken*
o	odd	ng	ring	i	in *possible*
ō	open	th	thin	o	in *melon*
				u	in *circus*

thumb /thum/
1. *noun* The short, thick finger on each hand.
2. *verb* To turn over pages.

tick·le /tik əl/ *verb*
1. To keep touching or poking gently, often causing someone to laugh. **2.** To have a tingling feeling.

ti·ger /tī gər/ *noun*
A large, striped, wild cat that lives in Asia. The tiger is the largest member of the cat family.

tim·ber /tim bər/ *noun*
1. Cut wood used for building. **2.** A long, heavy piece of wood; a beam. **3.** Trees; forest.

ti·ny /tī nē/ *adjective* Very small.

tire·less /tīr lis/ *adjective*
1. Never becoming tired or weak. **2.** Never stopping.

tire·less·ly /tīr lis lē/ *adverb*
In a tireless manner; without stopping.

toad /tōd/ *noun*
An animal that looks like a frog but has a rougher, drier skin. Toads live mainly on land. **Toad** sounds like **towed**.

tooth·brush /tooth brush/ *noun*
A small brush that is used to clean the teeth.

tough /tuf/ *adjective*
1. Strong and difficult to damage. **2.** Hard to cut or chew. **3.** Difficult to deal with or do. **4.** Able to stand strain or hardship.

towed /tōd/ *verb*
Pulled or dragged by a rope or chain. The past tense of **tow**. **Towed** sounds like **toad**.

tow·el /tou əl/ *noun*
A piece of soft cloth or paper that is used for drying or wiping.

tow·er /tou ər/
1. *noun* A tall structure that is thin in relation to its height. **2.** *verb* To be very tall.

trad·ed /trād əd/ *verb*
Exchanged one thing for another. Past tense of **trade**.

trad·ing /trād ing/ *verb*
Exchanging one thing for another.

traf·fic /traf ik/ *noun* Moving vehicles.

trea·sure /trezh ər/
1. *noun* Gold, jewels, money, or other valuable things.
2. *verb* To love and value something very highly.
▶ *verb* treasuring, treasured

trem·ble /trem bəl/ *verb*
1. To shake, especially from cold, fear, or excitement.
2. To quiver or quake. ▶ trembling, trembled

trou·ble /tru bəl/
1. *noun* A difficult, dangerous, or upsetting situation.
2. *verb* To disturb or worry someone. **3.** *noun* A cause of difficulty, worry, or annoyance. ▶ *verb* troubling, troubled

tru·ly /troo lē/ *adverb*
1. In a true way; sincerely. *I am truly sorry.* **2.** In fact; really. *He is truly the nicest person I know.*

tum·ble /tum bəl/ *verb*
1. To fall suddenly and helplessly. **2.** To do acrobatic feats. ▶ tumbling, tumbled

tu·na /too nə/ *noun* A large ocean food fish.

twin·kle /twing kəl/
1. *verb* To shine with quick flashes of light; to sparkle.
2. *noun* a flash of light. ▶ *verb* twinkling, twinkled

U u

un·a·ble /un ā bəl/ *adjective*
Cannot do something.

un·beat·en /un bēt ən/ *adjective*
Always a winner.

un·com·mon /un kom ən/ *adjective*
Rare or unusual; out of the ordinary.

un·fair·ly /un fâr lē/ *adverb*
In a way that is not fair or just.

un·fin·ished /un fin isht/ *adjective*
Not complete.

un·for·tu·nate /un fôr chə nit/ *adjective*
Unlucky.

un·hap·py /un hap ē/ *adjective*
1. Without joy. 2. Not lucky or fortunate.

un·kind /un kīnd/ *adjective* Not kind; mean.

un·known /un nōn/ *adjective*
Not familiar; not known about.

un·luck·y /un luk ē/ *adjective*
1. Unfortunate. 2. Having bad luck.

un·pleas·ant·ly /un plez ənt lē/ *adverb*
In a way that is not pleasing or agreeable.

un·u·su·al /un yōō zhōō əl/ *adjective*
Not usual, common, or ordinary; rare.

un·wrap /un rap/ *verb*
To take the packaging or outer layer off something.
▶ **unwrapping, unwrapped**

use·ful /yōōs fəl/ *adjective*
Helpful and can be used a lot.

use·less /yōōs lis/ *adjective*
Has no use or value.

 V v

va·ca·tion /vā kā shən/ *noun*
A time of rest from school, work, and so on, possibly to travel.

 W w

waf·fles /wäf əlz/
noun, plural Crisp batter cakes having a crisscross pattern in them. *I like to eat waffles and syrup for breakfast.*

wa·gon /wag ən/ *noun*
1. A vehicle with four wheels that is used to carry loads. 2. A child's toy vehicle with a long handle.

waist /wāst/ *noun*
1. The middle part of the body between the ribs and hips. 2. The part of a garment that covers the waist. **Waist** sounds like **waste**.

wait /wāt/ *verb* 1. To stay in a place until something happens. 2. To look forward to something. **Wait** sounds like **weight**.

warm·er /wôrm ər/ *adjective* A little hotter.

warm·est /wôrm ist/ *adjective* Hottest.

waste /wāst/
1. *verb* To use or spend something carelessly.
2. *noun* Garbage; something left over and not needed. **Waste** sounds like **waist**.

wa·ter·mel·on /wô tər mel ən/ *noun*
A large, juicy fruit that grows on vines.

wealth·y /wel thē/ *adjective*
Having a lot of money, property, or other valuables.

a	add	ô	order	th	this
ā	ace	oŏo	took	zh	vision
â	care	ōō	pool		
ä	palm	u	up		
e	end	û	burn	ə	=
ē	equal	yōō	fuse	a	in *above*
i	it	oi	oil	e	in *sicken*
ī	ice	ou	pout	i	in *possible*
o	odd	ng	ring	o	in *melon*
ō	open	th	thin	u	in *circus*

weath·er /weth ər/ *noun*
The condition of the outside air or atmosphere at a particular time and place.

weigh /wā/ *verb* **1.** To measure how heavy or light someone or something is by using a scale. **2.** To have a particular weight. **Weigh** sounds like **way**.

weight /wāt/ *noun* **1.** The measure of how heavy someone or something is. **2.** A unit used for measuring weight. **Weight** sounds like **wait**.

wet·ter /wet ər/ *adjective* Damper.

wet·test /wet ist/ *adjective* Dampest.

whis·tle /wis əl/ **1.** *noun* An instrument that makes a high, shrill, loud sound when you blow it. **2.** *verb* To make such a sound by blowing air through your lips. ▶ *verb* whistling, whistled

wife /wīf/ *noun* The female in a marriage.

wig·gle /wig əl/ *verb*
To make small movements from side to side or up and down. ▶ wiggling, wiggled

wind **1.** /wīnd/ *verb* To wrap something around something else. **2.** /wīnd/ *verb* To twist and turn. **3.** /wind/ *noun* Moving air. ▶ *verb* winding, wound

win·dy /wind ē/ *adjective* Having wind.

win·ter /win tər/ *noun* The season between autumn and spring; the coldest season.

win·try /win trē/ *adjective*
1. Of or like the winter. **2.** Chilly.

wise /wīz/ *adjective* Knowing or showing intelligence.

with·drawn /with drôn or with drôn/ *adjective*
Very shy and quiet.

wives /wīvz/ *noun* The plural of **wife**.

wolf /woolf/ **1.** *noun* A wild mammal that looks like the dog. **2. Idiom:** To **cry wolf** means to give a false alarm to get attention.

wolves /wulvz/ *noun* The plural of **wolf**.

won·der·ful /wun dûr fəl/ *adjective*
Causing wonder, remarkable, amazing.

worth·less /wûrth lis/ *adjective*
Has no value or is useless.

wound /wound/ *verb* **1.** Wrapped something around something else. Past tense of **wind** /wīnd/.

writ·ten /rit ən/ *verb*
Had put down on paper. ▶ write, writing, wrote

wrote /rōt/ *verb* Put down on paper. Past tense of **write**.

xy·lo·phone /zī lə fōn/ *noun*
A musical instrument with bars that are struck to give different notes.

your·self /yûr self/ *pronoun* Your own self.

your·selves /yûr selvz/ *pronoun*
Your own selves. The plural of **yourself**.

ze·bra /zē brə/ *noun.* A wild animal similar to a horse with black and white stripes.

ze·ro /zir ō/ *noun*
1. The numeral 0. **2.** A point on a scale at which measurement begins.

zip·per /zip ər/ *noun*
A fastener for clothes with interlocking metal teeth.

zoo /zoo/ *noun* A nature preserve.